I

"THE FORGOTTEN POWER"

FIRST PUBLISHED BY JOHN JOSEPH MANNING ce - MARCH 2002.

PERMISSIONS

95% of Scriptures quoted are taken from the **HOLY BIBLE, NEW INTERNATIONAL VERSION**. Copyright C 1973, 1978, 1984 by International Bible Society. Used by permission of Hodder and Stoughton Limited.

Other versions quoted are from every Bible I have ever read, and I recall some quotes from the following:- The Catholic edition of the Good News Bible. The Holy Spirit Bible. New American Standard Bible Open Bible Edition.

"The Modern Catholic Encyclopedia" Published in Ireland by Gill & Macmillan Ltd. Dublin Ireland, Extracts with permission, January 2002.

"The English translation of the **Catechism of the Catholic Church** is copyright (for Ireland) 1994 Veritas Publications and Libreria Editrice Vaticana. All rights reserved". Extracts with permission granted February 2002.

"The Documents of Vatican II" Flannery Edition. Dominican Publications, Parnell Sq., Dublin 1. Extracts with permission granted, February 2002.

137,380
£10-00

This Book is dedicated to the memory of Dennis and Esther Manning my mam and dad who were great parents to me and my brothers and sisters. I also remember Mary my only living aunt and her husband now deceased Charles Voos and all deceased aunts and uncles. There were ten of us living, at the time mam and dad died (the eleventh was a still birth, way back). My dad told me he carried my mother on the crossbar of his new bicycle to Hollis St. Hospital, in Dublin, at two a.m. in the morning where one of us was born. I am not sure which of us it was. I do know it was not me. I also recall in memory my grandmother Mary Kelly, who was just wonderful and my grandad who often took me for walks in the woods at Garryard, Naas, Co. Kildare, before he died when I was five. This book is also dedicated to the memory of my wife Dolores' mam dad and family, living and dead. To all of the people I have met outside of the prayer groups and at prayer groups down through the years here and in other countries. To anyone I have hurt in anyway from the time that I can remember from my school days, and during my business years, please forgive me. To FR. PATRICK COLLINS C.M. who was the first person I ever met that was in the Spirit. I had received the Holy Spirit prior to meeting Pat, I knew he was Spirit filled and by the power of the Holy Spirit I could believe all he taught me on my journey to where I am today. I kept going back for more. I have read most of his books on the Holy Spirit, attended a lot of his seminars, bought hundreds of his little leaflets on the Holy Spirit etc. to give away to other people. I spoke with him recently and told him he never taught me anything, the pause of a few seconds

The Forgotten Power

The Power to Cope

John Manning
Catholic Evangelist

seemed like a half hour. However the things you told me, were confirmed by the Holy Spirit within me. Thank you. Never did you say anything to me that I could not find in Scripture.

I also want to thank all of the people past and present at UCB Radio, Stoke on Trent, England and Martin Purnell for giving me time slots from time to time and allowing me share my testimony on numerous occasions. I also want to thank Morgan McStay who wrote the foreword for this book and for his encouragement and sharing over the years and for his wife Pat for the cups of tea, and all of the following:- The Full Gospel Business Men's Fellowship International. Bro. Sean Fleming, Lexian Bothers, Drumcondra, Dublin, 9. Near FM Radio, Coolock, Dublin, for allowing me and Paul Mangan share the "God Talk" programme on two Sundays of each month, to which we get a good response.

Photography for cover by FINN O'CONNELL - Cover design by BRENDAN CULLEN.

To protect the privacy of some individuals whose testimonies are recorded in this book, names, addresses, of persons and places and other details have in a few places been changed.

IIII

or any of the old established Christian churches over the head. There is no love in that. I would also like to thank the following for helping me and guiding me through the start up times when I could not type or use the computer. Padraigh Kilbride - Mai and Brida Kelly - Patricia Kelly of Drumcondra. - Alma Hobson - Gene Fitzgerald - Declan and Betty Clancy - Jimmy Dempsey and his wife Lucy - Michael Garde - Liam Skelly and his wife Mary - Jim Sherlock for allowing me share my testimony on the Christian radio a few years back - I remember Kay Doyle now deceased who gave me my first pocket size Bible. I thank Fr. Aidan Carroll for allowing me share my testimony from the pulpit of the University church Dublin, where I had served Mass for most of my young life as a school boy, and other priests who allowed me share from their pulpits in the past here and in other countries. To Frances Hogan who brought the Old Testament alive for me in her Bible teaching classes - Gerry O'Connor - Olly Buckley - Paula Larkin - Jack O'Donoghue and his wife Margaret - Ron Price and his wife Janet of Worcester, Birmingham, England. - Charles   Willliams and his wife Ola, Orlando, Florida, USA.

The biggest **thank you** of all has to go to my wife Dolores that I love dearly for having the patience to put up with me. For being a great wife and mother, and when I am not there, for answering the phone and praying with people who need a chat. To my five children who have also being loving and caring to Dolores and me and to people who might call on the phone when Dolores and I are away and take messages.

V

$\mathcal{John}\ \mathcal{Manning}$

Matt. 10/7-8

(a)

Freely, Freely you have received

Freely, Freely give,

go in my name and because you believe,

others will know that I live.

*The people of the testimonies in this book
believed my story. Like the villagers believed
the story of the woman at the well in John 4/7
when she told them who she was speaking to.*

(b)

*Here I am Lord, I heard you calling in the
night.*

(A /B - Words taken from two of my favourite songs)

IN THIS BOOK

I share with you

MY PERSONAL EXPERIENCE BEFORE AND AFTER MY BAPTISM IN THE HOLY SPIRIT AND MY OBSERVATIONS SINCE THEN

(The Holy Spirit is a person, the third person of the trinity, my comforter and companion, who leads me into spiritual truth and revelation)

WHO HAS BEEN GIVEN TO ME

John Manning

who found it hard to cope.

The Holy Spirit is available to all who ask, in God's time.

A petrol engine will not run on diesel fuel.

The Holy Spirit can only move, when God's Word is spoken by a Spirit filled person.

The gifts are for all, male or female, denomination or not, Jew or Gentile. God sent His Word that is timeless to heal us. This is what is written in Isaiah 55/11. "That it will not return to me empty, but will accomplish what I desire and achieve the purpose for which I sent it" (I believe this refers to those that are born again). God will not watch over **PIOUS OPINIONS.** He will watch over **HIS WORD** that becomes the sword of the Spirit, a person, that we send back to Him when we pray. God's Word and promises will be fulfilled and sustained by the Holy Spirit the third person of the Trinity. *People NOT in the Spirit speak a dead word, they inform and leave disillusioned people.* Those *IN* the Spirit transform, when they speak the living Word, Gods' Word . . . *NOW* you can expect miracles.

***

You cannot draw money from your bank account if you do not have your pin number.

I AM *NOT* TELLING PEOPLE WHAT THEY SHOULD BELIEVE, HOW TO PRAY, OR WHAT GOD TO BELIEVE IN.

(Man's Vocation page 391-*174:* Life in the Spirit. Catechism of the Catholic Church, pocket edition*)*

"GOD WILLED THAT MAN SHOULD BE LEFT IN THE HAND OF HIS OWN COUNSEL, SO THAT HE MIGHT AT HIS OWN ACCORD SEEK HIS CREATOR AND FREELY ATTAIN HIS FULL AND BLESSED PERFECTION BY CLEAVING TO HIM".

I, AND THE PEOPLE OF THE TESTIMONIES SHARED IN LOVE, ARE TELLING THOSE INTERESTED, HOW WE COPED AFTER GOD, THE FATHER OF THE TRINITY HEARD OUR PRAYER.

THE GOD OF UNCONDITIONAL LOVE WHO LOVES YOU WHETHER YOU LOVE HIM OR NOT. GOD HAS GIVEN EVERY HUMAN BEING THE GIFT OF FREE WILL TO PRAY, WORSHIP AND FOLLOW ANY DOCTRINE OR GOD HE/SHE WISHES TO FOLLOW.

Contents

CHAPTER 1

True testimonies.

Pages 1 to 57

The testimony of John and Dolores Manning, covers business problems and debts. Sickness of a crippling nature, elopement and bereavement, and coping with a special needs child named Amanda. Her mam and I the grandad, prayed in the intensive care unit of the Rotunda Hospital Dublin, on the first day of her life. We did not know if she was going to live or die. I read the Scriptures to her every day for a period of six months until she was transferred to ICU, Temple Street, Dublin. The Scripture reading continued on a daily basis for another five months until she came home for her first birthday. Join us on this journey if you wish.

Pages 58 to 105

The testimony of Paul and Catherine, covers drugs, infant and adult death, unforgiveness, loneliness and guilt.

x

Contents

True testimonies continued.

Pages 106 to 193

The seven a.m. hitch hiker. *A healing and conversion prayer for people in bereavement, caused by the death of loved one, or someone you they did not love. *The story of the pub theologian, who asked was Eve having sex with her sons and practising incest. *The layman's role and what Vatican II says about it. *The testimony of Dolores Manning who was healed from rheumatoid arthritis, for reasons that only God knew in advance about and which is revealed in baby Amanda's story. *The story of Susie from Albany, N.Y who was cured of Mylocytic Leukemia. *Una should be belly up in the canal behind Croke Park. *Anne suicidal ready to jump from four floors up. *Kay Abortion flash backs. *Sarah was told by her dad that she and her sisters were ugly. *The beggar man who was always caught robbing. *The dog was saved so was her marriage. *David was blind but could see. *They missed their plane to Australia, so they thought. *I enjoyed my posh lunch and my friend had indigestion. *The woman who was uninvited listened in and was healed. *The story of the oxygen mask. *He believes marriages can be made in hell. * Sean tells us about the death of his wife and his own illness. *The healing of the person on the life support machine within a few hours to pulling the plug. *She was a nurse, a drug addict from medication, an alcoholic and also had an out of body experience. *The story of the Woman at the post/mail box, Dublin 9, Ireland and the questions she asked and the answers I gave her. *She pulled back the curtains after years, her story reminded me of that great classic called "Great expectations". *Two ordinary joes looking for a dig out. *Amanda who is eight cannot walk or talk and is tube fed, tells us her story with her eyes and body language what love is. *Is the cause of your loneliness listed between page 183 and 194 ?

CHAPTER 2

Pages 194 to 328

Controversial because I ask why the teachings given me by my church and school were not in keeping with Scripture. As Vatican II, The Catechism of the Catholic Church and Modern Catholic Encylopedia teach.

I John Manning share with the reader, in the following pages the things that I believe cause and prevent signs and wonders. I try to separate truth, fiction, pious opinions, heresy, wrong beliefs etc. and ask many questions in love, believing from my proven experience how the old established Institutional churches got it wrong, particularly the one I was born and incorporated into. * Can you cope with your loneliness and the cause ? * Is the cause of your loneliness mentioned ? check the pages and see ? and what are you going to do about it ? * Has the bible a place in the world to day ? * Does infant baptism make you a Christian ? * Who said we are the devils children ? * Who said we have itching ears ? * Who says we babble like pagans ? * Why no rosary for priests ? * How I pray and what I say to mammies and daddies whose children or family were murdered or committed suicide ? * The prayers I say with mammies who have had abortions, miscarriages, still births etc.? * The prayers I say with people trying to stay off the drink, or give up gambling.

CHAPTER 3

Pages 329-435

Contents controversial because some of the things that I was told to believe contradict scripture.

The questions people ask and the answers I gave. *The following are extracts.* Was Mary the mother of Jesus a sinner ? Will I go to heaven when I die ? Does Limbo and Hell exist ? Is the Devil real ? Does purgatory exist ? Why does God cause suffering ? Was Darwin right ? Was there a famine in Ireland, why did God allow it ? Where do people who are not Roman catholic go when they die ? My son is gay, will he go to hell when he dies ? If there is only one true church how come we have so much division ?

Special prayer pages

For those bereaved, for those with disabilities, for mammies who have had abortions, miscarriages or still births. Pages 330/31 prayer for those contemplating divorce or separation. Pages 339/40/41 for families of suicide victims. Page 357 for those who have lost their virginity. Page 355 for those where mam and dad are separating. Pages 348/349 sex and marriage. Pages 350/51/52 for gamblers. Pages 361/62/63 prayer for alcoholics who are on the dry but cannot find peace. Page 355 for those contemplating divorce or separation. Pages 406/7 for parents whose children are in jail. Pages 268/73 for those that have had to live with domestic violence and how to pray around it. Page 410 a prayer for those who are being bullied. Pages 417/18/19 a prayer for those who feel that the love for their husband/wife has gone cold. *Pages 429/30 the healing and conversion prayer.*

FOREWORD

I first met John Manning many years ago in a group of Roman Catholic people who had like both of us experienced a profound conversion to personal faith in Jesus and baptism in the Holy Spirit. This experience was shared by many thousands of people in the different Christian Churches, in a move of the Holy Spirit in Ireland, which began in the early 1970s. We now realise that even though this personal life transforming event took place outside the formal structures of the Churches, it was nevertheless completely in line with scripture.

Scripture tells us that before Jesus ascended into Heaven He instructed His disciples to remain in Jerusalem until they received power from above. On the day of the first Christian Pentecost the Apostles and the other people assembled in the upper room received the baptism of the Holy Spirit, as promised by Jesus. They also received the gifts of the Holy Spirit in accordance with the Lord's will and were empowered for the tasks ahead. The Holy Spirit subsequently raised up many to perform the ministries of Apostle, Prophet, Pastor, Teacher and Evangelist, for the purpose of building up the Body of Christ, which is the church. The baptism of the Holy Spirit and the gifts and ministries of the Holy Spirit were not just intended for the infant Church; they were the Lords provision for the Church in every age. I believe that they are the spiritual marks of normal Christian Church life.

John Manning and I became close friends and he often shared about his own walk with the Lord and what was happening in his ministry. In this book he tells the story of his own remarkable journey to personal faith in Jesus and of his calling by the Holy Spirit to share that living faith with others, as an Evangelist.

Scripture states that the gospel is the power of God for salvation and that faith comes by hearing the word of God. With the light and guidance of the Holy Spirit, John has faithfully accepted and boldly applied the wisdom of Holy Scripture, the living word of God, to his ministry with amazing results.

Over the years John has encountered most of the problems that trouble people today and he has been asked to address many spiritual questions. His practice has always been to prayerfully turn first to the scriptures for guidance and insight and then to speak plainly and directly. He has the ability to connect with people and to communicate with them at the deepest level. He has never been afraid to confront error wherever he finds it. The touching personal testimonies of the many people featured in this book are a powerful affirmation of his ministry.

Despite the recent fall off in church attendance there is a great spiritual hunger in those outside the experience of God's love. John Manning is a remarkable man of God with a remarkable desire to satisfy that hunger by introducing people to Jesus and to witness the power of the Holy Spirit at work in their lives.

This book is not a work of theology, it is the story of a man coming to personal faith in Jesus and what happened when he allowed the Holy Spirit to empower and guide his ministry as an Evangelist. It will inspire, and offer help and comfort to many people in need, and it will point the way to Jesus.

If the churches are in decline today it is because the gifts and ministries of the Holy Spirit, which are the Lord's provision for building up the Body of Christ, are not being exercised. These gifts and ministries are not optional.

I believe the time has come for the present leadership in all the Christian Churches to recognise and affirm the sovereign work of the Holy Spirit, as He raises up women and men such as John Manning from the ranks of the ordinary people of God, and equips them for ministry within the body of Christ.

Morgan Mc Stay
Dublin, March, 2002

A number of years ago, while minding my own business in every sense of the word the

God of the living

(THOSE BORN AGAIN AND BAPTISED IN THE HOLY SPIRIT)

interrupted my life

My testimony covers business debts, the fear of going bust, sickness, disabilities of a crippling nature, elopement, bereavement, and caring for a special needs child.

State and industry need the self-employed entrepreneurs, yet there are no benefits if you go bust, your family and yourself carry the can.

my Journey starts *now*

Why not join me ?
What happened to me and others can happen to
you!

"Here, John, read this book when you get a chance. I think that organisation would suit you because of your kind nature". I thanked my friend, a very glamorous lady, who was Managing Director of a successful business. I put the book in my pocket and went on my way. Work, golf and money was my new god. I was a millionaire in the making, or so I thought.

If you want to read on you are welcome !

Six months later I read the book "Voice Magazine" – for so it was titled – and loved every bit of it. Stories short and sweet, as easily read as "The Readers Digest". It told the stories of men and women of all denominations who meet and discuss what God has done and was doing in their lives, in relation to miracles, signs and wonders. My good intention, however, of putting the thought of turning to God into action was shelved indefinitely.

Approximately seven years later I heard by accident that the Full Gospel Business Men's Organisation were having a healing meeting like I had read about seven years earlier in a hotel on the north side of

Dublin. I went along accompanied by my wife Dolores, who was almost confined to bed from crippling rheumatoid arthritis. There were fifty or sixty people present, husbands and wives, single people, male and female, all with their hands in the air singing loudly. After a sudden silence of maybe two minutes or so they all started praying in words Dolores and I had never heard before.

Eventually, there was a call for people to come forward for prayer. I remember so well three women in particular, told us they had cancer and were going up for prayer hoping to be healed. Some of the people present who were prayed over, fell to the ground as if they just fainted, and after a while got to their feet feeling good; unhurt by the fall they returned to their respective places, beside spouses or friends. A man by the name of Al Ryan, a healing evangelist was the main speaker that night, he and his wife Peg have been a great help to Dolores and I over the years. I thank them both, and I know the Lord has blest them in their ministry.

Dolores and I had never experienced this type of happening before. We weren't impressed and found it a bit scary to say the least. I was very anxious to get Dolores home as it was well past her bed time which was usually at nine thirty p.m.– the days were long and painful. By now it was getting on for twelve thirty a.m. All our friends can testify to the fact that my wife Dolores was full of arthritis from head to toe, bound up in pain and most uncomfortable if she sat or stood for too long. In fact, simple things like driving a car combing her hair, going to the bathroom, having a shower, putting on clothes, tights, shoes etc. were extremely difficult for her; even getting in and out of a car – so simple an action if one is mobile.

Next morning over breakfast we discussed, in between phone calls, the happenings of the evening before. We had gone to the meeting hoping that maybe God would touch Dolores somehow and that she would be healed. You will gather by now that nothing at all happened to Dolores' condition, and the fact that our children were not in full employment, I felt we were sitting on a bomb. All the money I had borrowed to get my business off the ground was gone. I could not raise any more even though I had good products and lots of stock that was paid for, but I found it difficult to sell. I had in the past dealt with businessmen of the sole proprietor family type helping with boardroom squabbles etc. as a referee and a problem solver. Now it looked as if I myself might not survive.

I am not a quitter, but the situation was getting to me mentally, physically, financially and spiritually. The prayers said were not working, I decided to visit my doctor for my monthly check up. I was on hypertension tablets a long while because of all the pressure I was under, a monthly check up was essential.

As I went out my front gate the postman arrived and handed me a letter containing a cheque I had figured I would never get - money from a State Organisation to fund a visit to the U.S.A. to attend a product familiarisation course.

God bless the mail/post man

I had the agency for particular products that had great potential in Ireland and mainland Europe. Excited by the arrival of the cheque, I ran upstairs to my wife Dolores and asked her to come with me to the U.S.A.

my telephone orders with them and I also learned a lot about their products and them as individuals. There was a bond between us even though we had never met. To our astonishment, on entering the passenger arrival section in our special courtesy car provided for Dolores we were confronted by a big poster bearing the words, "Welcome to Orlando John and Dolores".

"Welcome to Orlando, John and Dolores".

Our reception and all that happened subsequently confirmed the reputation of Americans for incomparable generosity. Our hosts offered us the hospitality of their home; but we opted instead for a nearby motel as I had to have receipts etc. as to how I spent the grant money. I also considered it a more diplomatic arrangement in view of our mutual involvement in the pending negotiations, which could possibly culminate in the buying out of the company I was to visit (management buy out) not by Dolores and me but by other people working for the company. In my old business over the years, I had dealt with take-overs, buy-outs etc., private and public; they are all the same – agro and hassle. I was picked up at six a.m. daily to go to the laboratory to study the products I would have to market and sell in Europe. The people at the motel where we stayed were just fantastic, they looked after Dolores every day, brought her food etc., while I was working at the laboratory.

Dolores was treated like a queen !

Occasionally, when Dolores was up to it people from the laboratory took us to dinner. One night they brought us to a healing prayer meeting where people prayed with Dolores for healing. Yet, nothing happened, although things appeared to be happening to other people all around us. Dolores and I did not seem to get the message at all. We were just immune to everything. We couldn't fail to notice how so many successful, highly qualified business people, men and women, of different denominations were united in their effort to know God better and develop their relationship with Him, which was rather strange to us as I didn't know if God was there or not. I was told he was.

The chief chemist of the company I represented in Europe, was a professor and top adviser to the US oil industry and government and the author of many books and was involved in the Roman Catholic Charismatic Renewal in the USA. The president of the company was an elder in the Assemblies of God Church, one of the fastest growing Churches in America. These are but two examples, both reminiscent of what we had experienced in Dublin seven years earlier at a similar type of interdenominational meeting.

Still no healing for Dolores

No healing for Dolores, we left Florida after three weeks intensive product training. Dolores in a lot of pain despite painkillers and prayer we set off on the second part of our journey to Kentucky University, where our daughter, Amanda, lived and was studying. We stayed with her and her husband, Patrick, who took very good care of us and provided a wheelchair for Dolores. One evening they invited several young people around to dinner. After a lovely meal we sat out on the deck at the back of the house and had home-made ice cream for dessert. We enjoyed watching the fireflies lighting up the darkness and speculating on their amazing capacity to produce fluorescent lighting. As the evening went on, we became more and more aware of how nice the young couples were and then discovered that their parents were all Christian missionaries in different parts of the world. Greatly impressed, I was beginning to ask myself about this Christian bit versus Roman Catholic bit. Slow as it was in coming there was something happening at last. It reminded me of a friend who said he had dancing in his blood but bad circulation prevented it from getting to his feet. After ten days, which we enjoyed, and watching the supply of pain killers go down, we set off for New York to our other daughter who was getting engaged.

We were met in New York by our daughter Anne Mariae, her intended Christopher Stosiek and Christopher's father, Martin. After three hours driving we arrived in Hillsdale, New York, the native place of Anne Mariae's future in-laws.

The next day was Sunday and a new surprise awaited us; when we went to Mass at St. Bridget's Church we were greeted by Father Peter and Mr. Stosiek dressed in deacon's garb – our first experience of a deacon in the Roman Catholic Church.

The action brought tears to my eyes

As the priest, Father Peter, lifted up the Host during the mass at the elevation, Mrs. Stosiek stretched across me, took Dolores' hand and prayed in some strange language like we had heard at the Dublin and Florida meeting. Such an act of love brought tears to our eyes. Since our arrival in America we were being bombarded by love from people we hardly knew from different backgrounds, churches religions and denominations.

Eventually they eloped and saved me a fortune,
that I did not have.

We arrived in Hillsdale, New York, from Kentucky just in time for the engagement party for our daughter Anne Mariae to Christopher Stosiek and they would be married within two years they said, so we gave them our blessing and enjoyed the party. Not knowing then that they would elope and be married within twelve months. However we coped.

They got married in a church near Great Barrington, Mass. USA. A priest friend of theirs said the mass and performed the ceremony. It was not a shot gun affair as some people might have thought. Christopher and Anne did not want to cause Dolores and me any hassle, knowing Dolores' health and my financial situation. They phoned both sets of parents after the wedding and through the tears Dolores and I heard the story. We congratulated them and said that was ok. We left you and Christopher, and all our other children and family in the Lord's hands every day, and if the Lord allowed this to happen, fine.

In order that our return journey to Ireland would be as comfortable as possible for Dolores who was now showing the worst of the wear, I was anxious to fly directly from New York to Dublin. The airline we were booked on out of New York was not going to Shannon or Dublin but to London. As we left our daughters home to go to New York airport, I felt Dolores would not be able for the journey – New York – London – Dublin as she was quite bad. I decided to pray, even though I had not a bull's notion how to do so. I said "dear Jesus, if you are as good as the others say you are, would you ever ask God to do something about getting us to Dublin direct from New York with Aer Lingus even though we have Pan Am tickets". Would Aer Lingus accept the

Pan Am tickets if I went to the people in charge and explained about Dolores' health. After Dolores and I had a chat with a member in charge at Pan Am, I hoped they would agree New York to Dublin was the way to go for Dolores having witnessed her condition.

London was no problem, London to Dublin was because of the two hour wait in London, coupled with jet lag would make it very rough for Dolores.

The hard neck and cheek you need to stay in business allowed me approach both airlines, and tell my story to someone in management. We came into New York early so as that I could check things out. After a few meetings with people from both airlines, Aer Lingus, God bless them, came back and said that they would accept the other airline's tickets if there was a seat. No extra charges, we had no money and no connections. I got more adventurous and braver with God now, and said "surely Jesus you can go all the way now and get us a seat, even though I am not sure where you are or if you are there". Ten minutes before the gates closed for the flight to Dublin with Aer Lingus we were called to board. I said to Dolores as we boarded, "Jesus is me man". We arrived home safely. Before we went to the USA, I was up to my neck in debt, with this new business that was going to make me a millionaire. I was miles overdrawn, no money, only potential, no children's allowance, no nothing. My stock was all paid for, VAT, duty etc., however, I could not give the product away. On paper I believed I was a winner. Now here I was faced with maybe selling my house, surrendering my life policies and me paying twice the normal premium per thousands pounds of cover, because of my hypertension which I had for fourteen years and bordering on being uninsurable. If my health did not improve, if I could not stay in business, how embarrassing for me, my family and mam an invalid, five children and not a bob to rent a caravan or tent. When you are self-employed you have to survive, there are no benefits.

I closed the offices I had in town to cut down on my overheads. I often sat at home pondering on things, me the great survivor now up to my neck in trouble. I remember so well sitting in my office at home before, and after our trip, listening to Dolores trying to get to the bathroom or come down the stairs and calling out to God to help her with the pain.

Guilt sets in, I asked myself a million times "Why is everything happening now", I had never failed before here or in America where we lived for five years. Fear was over me like a black cloud. I was always taught as a young man to pray rosaries, novenas, light candles to this saint and that saint, go to mass and holy communion every day, the things I was brought up to rely on were not working. Now I know they never could. I was programmed wrong. As I set out each morning at six thirty for Cork, Limerick, Monaghan, Galway or Donegal the five children looked after themselves and got ready for school. I would try to make Dolores comfortable. Hit the road and not see them until I got home, eight at night would be early. Dolores despite her pain etc. was always cheerful. She would tell me what happened during the day. Mary Murphy our friend who has gone home to the Lord, might have made her weekly call, to take Dolores to the hairdressers like she had done for the last fifteen years of the forty we knew her. We miss her. Eamonn her husband might have come to fix the washing machine. Her sister Maura might have come down to give her a shower or body wash. Marie who lives next door, would bake apple pies, and her husband Paddy would hand them over the garden wall to one of the children. They always left the "da" a few slices, God bless them.

As I drove the roads, some good, some bad, all kinds of depressing things would cross your mind. One morning on my to the town of Tullamore from Portlaoise town a journey of a few miles, across a narrow road, with lots of ups and downs when I had to really hold on to the steering wheel. A big double trailer truck went by and as it did a big buckle on the canvas, struck the roof of my car and nearly put me off the road into the bog. It did cross my mind that had I gone, my troubles were over, so I journeyed on. The worries continued, like would I have enough petrol to get home, I hope Dolores does not fall down the stairs, I hope the children are ok. I hope I can survive and not go bust. I hope the people that I have appointments with today turn up. I wonder

137,380

why that man did not turn up this morning, he never left a message. I must be nuts, why did I start this business, I should never have allowed the Americans talk me into it. I should never have borrowed so much. Why was I not a guy in a secure job. Dolores and I having settled back into a routine, no different than before, still could not see any light. New ideas to promote my product were resumed. Driving home late one night, I recalled the hassle that went on in relation to the management buy out of the American company, and how I kept out of the politics of it all. I did not have enough background information to be able to judge what was what, or who was who. My thinking was confused; the ups and downs of the past, the grasping at any slight glimmer of hope for the future, the permanent image of Dolores with her crippling and deforming affliction, her continuous pain which affected every part of her body.

Why don't I live in that house where
the lights have just gone out?

Picture driving through the countryside late at night with the window of the car open in an effort to stay awake; you hear the merriment from the pubs; as you pass through towns and villages, you wearily observe the lights going off in houses as people went to bed. With eighty miles to go, you would give anything to be able to do the same thing yourself. But somehow I always did manage to get home safely, though often, I suspect, only by the grace of God, and sometimes with the help of a tail wind when petrol was low. Then I would wonder if I would be able to get up in the morning to set out for some other remote destination. I doubt if I could have survived those difficult times without the help of so many.

As I went through the post one day, right in the middle of all the bills was a notice from the Full Gospel Business Men's International, advertising a week end convention in Cork. Dolores saw the notice and hid it, but I found it and announced that we were going. Always practical, she said: "No. You do not have what would jingle on a tombstone; you can't afford to go anywhere". I wanted to go and talked her into it and set out for Cork on the new train – all on sixty pounds cash and a cheque to pay the hotel bill – all borrowed from my son John.

In Cork we registered in to the conference hotel, had a short rest followed by dinner and then found a safe spot in the conference room where Dolores would not be disturbed. There were about six hundred people present from all walks of life, among them priests and nuns, which I found reassuring. I was further encouraged on meeting an old friend, Jimmy a business associate whom I knew to be a good Roman Catholic.

As the meeting progressed and the singing ended, men got up at the top table and in turn told the gathering how they overcame drink, drugs, perversions of all kinds. Two of the men were from Brussels and held high positions in the law and accountancy professions, and a third was a pig farmer. Another was Charles Dukes, an astronaut who walked on the moon. I could see no difference between them and me in relation to problems, stress, strain, anxiety, etc. They seemed to have found a great peace, which was visible in them. This peace seemed to run through each of them like a thread through fabric. Men explained how they found peace, when they made Jesus Lord of their lives, they were able to come to grips with the day to day problems of life. It struck me that this Jesus I had heard about and did not know, was real to these people, and not on the cross-not dead but alive. I had never thought of Jesus as risen and alive – to me He was still on the cross or somewhere. Now I began to feel that, if he could help these people and lead them from darkness into light, perhaps He could do it for Dolores and me, and bring some relief with our health and money problems then maybe life would seem worth living.

It did not happen before we went to Florida or in Florida, Kentucky or New York despite all the praying.

The Altar call

Before the meeting ended, there was a procedure known as an altar call for those who wanted to submit their lives to Christ. Without making a conscious decision, I found myself talking to a lady named Pat Carver from California a Christian lady of another denomination, and Jim Fleming a great man in the Lord from Northern Ireland who took me aside for prayer. (I later discovered that Pat was a neighbour of ours when Dolores and I lived in California, we never met then, but we did twenty five years later in God's time). I told her before she prayed with me that I had not come to the convention in Blarney, Cork, Ireland, for myself, but for my wife, who was severely crippled with rheumatoid arthritis and would she come and pray with her. I have her tucked away at the back of the room in case someone might bump into her and knock her down. Pat said: "No, maybe the Lord wants to talk to you first." I explained that I was a practising Roman Catholic and had no intention of changing my religion. A beautiful smile, came across her face as she gently touched my forehead and said: "There are no denominations in Heaven only those that are born again". I didn't understand this born again bit!. A great peace came over me and I relaxed. I proceeded to tell Pat my story. I think she understood when I said I felt like the Jumbo Jet going out over the Atlantic. I was definitely gone past the point of no return.

I was beyond human help; there was no sense in borrowing more money, no one would give me any, simply because I would not be able to repay it. So I said to Pat: "I have been a good Roman Catholic all my life, served Mass for years and attended to all my religious duties and I am still not sure God is there. If He is I would like to know" and she said: "Well, we will ask Him".

As I closed my eyes and prayed, in a standing position, a great peace come over me, and I knew then that it was that peace that I had heard the people talk about. It was different from the way you feel, when you need money and someone pays you, that makes you happy, and brings peace for a while, like having nice clothes, money in the bank, of not being in the red, of going on a holiday with plenty of money. This was indeed a new feeling. It was like as if someone washed me down with a power hose from head to toe, it was a peace that stayed.

A beautiful rainbow

I had found that peace which defies all human understanding. It was just great, and I responded in my spirit by saying to God: "If this peace I have right now is you in me, I will work for You forever". I know now, that God had brought me close to Jesus His only son, who says "You cannot come to me unless my father draws you".

The minute I uttered these words, my eyes still closed, the vision of a rainbow appeared in front of me. It was just magnificent, in full colour and easy to look at; I will never forget it. And on one curve of this rainbow was my wife's head and shoulders, smiling and happy, looking as she does today as I share my experiences with you, not as she looked then, tired worn out and weary. On the curves underneath I saw the heads and shoulders of my five children, all with beautiful smiles.

As I came out of this great peace, the rainbow gone, I opened my eyes to discover that I was on the floor in a dazed condition, no bump, no reflex action. I got up and went to Dolores and told her what I had experienced, explained everything and said no more. Dolores went up the next night for prayer and she was slain in the Spirit (I know the name for it now). She did not have any vision. I phoned Charlie Williams at head office in Florida and told him of my experience, no knowing that half of the office staff and warehouse staff were listening in, all I could hear in the background was praise the Lord and all that stuff, they were all Christians. I now know that there is a difference between being a member of a denomination and a Christian. Then there was great silence on the phone and Charlie asked "John are you listening". I sure am I replied. Do you know what has happened to you, I said no, well he said when Noah saw the rainbow he knew God had kept His promise. Anything you ask God for John you will get when you pray in spirit and truth. You have had a mighty blessing you are born again and have received the Holy Spirit. The signs and wonders have happened. The more I told my story to people in groups or on the phone, someone was always healed or comforted in a big way. So the reason for writing this book is that I want others to do what I am doing, for there is a hunger out there.

I also found that I could now understand the scriptures though I was never trained.

Dolores was walking without pain

Within six months Dolores started to slowly get better and I would say is now 99% recovered. She can walk freely without pain. Health problems I had myself since then were treated successfully by medication and prayers. I had my life insurance re-evaluated and got normal life insurance rates. I had no more need for hypertension tablets – I was healed. Each time that I faced a test under anaesthetic for biopsies, I turned to prayer, asking the Lord to bind the spirit of fear in me and set me free. Never after that was I afraid; I never lost the peace that defies all human understanding, which I received that night when I was baptised in the Holy Spirit. People would say to me: "That is a terrible cross you have to bear with your business problems, Dolores sick and you not well". I answered by saying "If you knew Christ, or if you ask Christ into your life as I did, you will cope. Make Jesus Lord of your life, and then the Holy Spirit lifts you above everything and nothing becomes a cross or a burden any more".

(Matt. 6/33)

But seek first His kingdom, and His righteousness, and all these things will be given to you as well.

(2 Cor. 4/3-4 Psalm 9/17- Iss. 5/13-14).

When the Gospel is hidden it leads to a Christ-less society, just look around you to day.

The gospel is veiled/hidden to those who are perishing. The god of this age, the devil, has blinded the minds of unbelievers so that they cannot see the light of the gospel of the glory of Christ, who is the image of God.

The Spirit teaches me all things!

and it has nothing what so ever to do with

denominations, as is explained clearly

in Hebrews 2/11-12-13-14

I believe revelation is better than theology. Divine grace is better than human ability. We hold intellectual education above character building, as you can experience in our society at all levels to day. We hold psychology above discernment. We hold programming above being guided by the Spirit. We hold laws above love, reasoning above walking in faith.

(Hebs.-2 - 11/12/13/14)

Tells me that we are the Father's children, given to His son, to be brothers and sisters in Christ.

As the weeks and months went by my level of faith was growing and only God can make it grow. I had developed a great hunger for the Word, which I believe is the way to happiness and inner peace. I was beginning to understand Scripture, not in the natural sense but through revelation; and the more I read the more I learned of God's mercy and his love for me, that unconditional, steadfast love that only He can give. Because of my coming to Christ, in my brokenness, my desire for any of those things St. Paul warns us against in Galatians 5/16-26 are not there any longer. They are: sexual immorality, impurity and debauchery, idolatry and witchcraft, hatred, discord, jealousy, fits of rage, selfish ambitions, dissension, factions and envy; drunkenness, orgies and the like. My life has turned around completely. I am happy and content; I just cannot imagine my living in any way other than in the Spirit. I will cope no matter what comes my way, *not knowing what was ahead.* Pray your way out of your situation. Do not wait until you are broken physically, spiritually, emotionally or financially. Ask Jesus into your life **now;** do not put it off.

Summing Up

1. I never lost my business
2. I never lost my house (that looked in jeopardy)
3. I sold my Mercedes, a pride thing.
4. Survived three rear end car accidents.
5. Hospitalised three times for biopsy's, all clear.
6. I suffer from Chronic Sinuses, not healed yet but it does not matter, God's grace is sufficient.
7. Dolores can walk again, no pain, no depression.
8. Assets greater than liabilities now.
9. Since I started writing this book I have had an Angiogram / Angioplasty. I thank God for the nurses and the Doctors. I am just great. I believe the reason I am still here is quite obvious. If you have the time read the story of "Dolores and Amanda" on pages 121 to 131.

Bereavement

Something every human being will experience.

**This testimony, of how I John Manning
coped with my mam and dad's death, may help you.
I share with you in love as I have with others
on our telephone help line, of over 2,360 families,
on radio, in churches and schools of
all denominations,
here and in other countries.**

My Dad was into astronomy, and knew a lot about the sun, moon and stars and all the planets, including the supposed birth place of the stars "Orion Nebula" and its location. During a discussion on the above a few days before he died, dad asked me "where was heaven-was it up, down, or suspended in space?"

"I do not know Dad!" "I replied, however, I will get my bible out of the car and see where God says it is". (as an evangelist it is important that I take myself out of the picture, and quote the Word of God. When I do, it becomes believable, by the power of the Spirit).

The same God that knew you by your name, before your mam and dad did, is the same God that can hold the sun, moon, stars and all the planets in the solar system in suspension, without visible means of support, no scaffolding, ladders or ropes.

Having returned with one of my Bibles from the car, the usual two to three hour Sunday tea session went on for hours. "Dad! this is what Scripture says about heaven and its location, relax now as I read it in 2 Cor. 12/2. "I know a man in Christ who fourteen years ago was caught up to the third heaven whether it was in the body or out of the body I do not know but God knows. The third heaven designates a place beyond the immediate heaven of the earth's atmosphere, where we live, and beyond the further heaven of outer space and constellations, into the presence of God himself. Where I believe all those who have died in Christ up to now are at home with the Lord.

Thus the risen and glorified Lord is said to have "passed through the heavens" having "ascended higher than all the heavens" then to be "exalted above the heavens". Dad, I believe that our spirit bodies will travel the same journey as Jesus, leave the earth's atmosphere as the angels take us up through the heavens, to the highest heaven where God says he dwells. Fine, he said, I know now that heaven is a place, not a state of mind, it is not below and not suspended. He got up from his chair, got out his maps of the solar system that he knew so well, and followed the directions given in the Scriptures as to where heaven is. He enjoyed the trip as I shared the map with him. Only God knew that he was going to die four days later when he travelled from the earth's atmosphere where we live, to the third heaven and into God's dwelling place.

I explained to mam and dad the journey and route I thought the Spirit body that never enters the coffin, would travel after physical death, to live forever outside of time.

So Dad, when my time comes, when Dolores' time comes, when your time comes mam and yours dad, God will lead us to green pastures. Where with the eyes of our spirit bodies, we can look out through the windows of heaven, and see all the planets in the heavens that fascinated you all of your life. You will be able to say, (1Cor. 15/55) "Where, O death, is your sting."

As the chat continued, I shared what the apostle Paul said, (Phil. 1/23) "For I am hard-pressed between the two, having the desire to depart (his spirit body from the physical body) and be with Christ, which is far better". "So dad and mam, we just have to stick it out no matter what our problem, just like Job and the Apostle Paul did. (Gal. 4/I3-14) I believe Paul felt rejected because he thought he was ugly, which I believe was the thorn in His flesh. So we hang in there until the Lord calls us home. Then our Spirit body that is perfect can return to God for reward or judgement".

(2 Sam. 12/18)

King David's son died

David said after his baby son died, that he would go to his son, and that his son could not return to him. Did he mean that he would go to visit his sons grave, or see him in heaven in the future? As I read this Scripture I thought of Lazarus and the rich man, no one is allowed to come back and tell us where they are, it all has to do with faith, you believe or you don't.

Mam, dad and I joined together on a few occasions in the past and said the conversion and healing prayer, when they became born again. They as adults repented, confirmed their baptismal vows, and accepted Jesus as their Lord and Saviour.

My dad's physical body died a few days after our Sunday chat, age eighty seven, and my mam nine months later at her age eighty seven. Life for them has not ended, but just begun.

We are made for the next world. Our spirit body is a living soul that is immortal and will never die. However our physical body which the spirit body indwells is mortal and will die ?

What a joy for Dolores and I, that God allowed us to share the same true story with my mam and dad on that Sunday before he died and with the people who were at both funeral masses, and with you, who might read this testimony.

Dundrum Roman catholic church, was full to capacity for both private masses.

There was a queue of people that I had never met, waiting to have a chat after each of the masses, regarding what I had said, people I did not know, the response was just great. Three of them said "Thank you for those consoling words, I am not afraid to die, my fear is gone. You answered a lot of questions for me, thank you". Other people gave a hug, shook hands or gave a kiss.

I miss my mam and dad, and I am happy that God took them home in His time, without too much suffering. In this world we only have a loan of one another.

My mam said before she died as my brothers, sisters and myself, stood around her bed in the hospital, waiting the arrival of our youngest brother Dennis from Australia, that he would be late and that she would see us all in heaven. I repeated to those present what she said, reminding them that because of our mam's relationship with Jesus, we in her household, may not avoid the pitfalls of life, but would be saved, given an opportunity to repent and be with her in heaven when our time comes. She and I often discussed the scriptures when she was alive, she just loved to listen to the Word as I read. She said it reminded her of the times her dad read and told her about Jesus as a young girl, now she understood. She died so peacefully as I said, "See you soon, mam", meaning that her spirit body and soul, like dads was outside of time now. I closed her eyes and whispered the living Word in her ear through tears of joy, no sadness because of what I know, I know. God's plan was complete for mam and dad.

Those that are left need prayer, not the people that are gone. We should thank God for our parents. My dad was fostered and never knew his parents. However, we still thanked God for them before he died and for the memories, good and bad and did not let the sun set on anger or unforgiveness.

We will all experience physical death?

Some people may never experience poverty, sickness, a broken marriage, or any of the awful problems we hear about today and that I have mentioned in this book. However, every human being like those of the past, present and to come, no exceptions, will experience physical death. By the grace of God I know – that my spirit body that is just like me, is a living soul, and not a piece of cotton wool, mist or cloud, and will go to heaven when my physical body dies. I also know, that I won't know I am there, until I arrive.

1/Thess. 5/23

(confirms for me what I understand about body soul and spirit)

"May God Himself, the God of peace, sanctify you through and through. May your whole spirit, soul and body be kept blameless at the coming of the Lord Jesus Christ. The one who calls you is faithful and He will do it".

Where will I go if I die? This crossed my mind a lot while in hospital waiting on results of tests.

I can go to bed now with no fear, or go under a full anaesthetic and say to God, if I wake up with you fine, if I wake up here that's fine also, you're the boss. I am in your hands.

I wait on God's promises to be fulfilled in Jesus' name as Jesus did. I thank God for the gift of a living faith that cannot be passed on. I am saddened from time to time when I hear it preached, that we should pass on the faith, you can pass on a doctrine but not faith in God, it is a gift to be asked for and received. Faith comes from hearing the Word of God. I thank God that I heard that Word.

My job as an evangelist, is not to please people, or judge, but to tell them about God's promises and his rest. As an evangelist, I can sow a seed, or water a seed that was sown by me or someone else, recently or in the distant past but only God can make it grow.

God says that "I change not (the Word from generation to generation) so you are not consumed, with fear and anxiety in the fires of hell. Every mass for me since my conversion is a joyous occasion. I love listening to the scriptures at mass and I take notes as the Holy Spirit reveals understanding. I believe it is a joyous time, a sacrifice of praise and thanksgiving, from the lips of those that have a personal relationship with Jesus, and not a blood sacrifice as some people in the Roman Catholic church and others believe and teach. I thanked the priest for allowing me share at my dad and mam's funeral mass, which was outside of the regular public mass time. Life is like a mist on the bog – we are here one minute and gone the next. We live in a time zone here on earth, where a thousand years is like one day in the next life.

Every day is exciting, I never know what is going to happen !

READ THE STORY OF THE WOMAN AT THE POST /MAIL BOX,
Mobhi Road, Dublin 9, Ireland.

On a beautiful day in September 1991, I was in the local post office buying some stamps when the post-mistress, whom I know well, asked me if I wanted a lotto ticket. I said, "No, God looks after all my needs". I did not know that a few people had formed a queue behind me and heard what I said. As I stood at the post box on the footpath sticking stamps on envelopes, a lady came over to me and said: "That was a lovely thing you said in the post office".

To make sure we were not on a crossed line, I asked her what I had said, "You said that God looks after all your needs". "And so He does", I replied. "Well, she said, "Why doesn't He look after all my needs?" Sure I go to Mass and Holy Communion every day of my life, but I have no peace. My husband is dead a few years and I often wonder if he will ever come back and tell me where he is; I have plenty of money; I live in a big house on my own". I began to wonder was she just "chatting me up"! My wife Dolores was sitting in the car, windows down listening to the conversation taking place as I was dropping letters into the post box.

I said to the lady "That is my wife whom I love dearly, and she can hear every word we say; and if my children find out that their dad was flirting with a good-looking widow in front of the ma, they won't take too kindly to it! I knew by then, the lady was very serious and quite concerned. The remarks made about Dolores and the children brought a smile to her face. I asked if she would like to say a prayer with me – remember we are standing on the footpath with lots of pedestrian traffic – she said she would love to say a prayer. I said "we will ask God who loves you unconditionally to bring you closer to Jesus – this will happen if you want it. Do you want it? "Yes", she said, "I do". I then went on to explain to her what I was going to do: "I will raise my right hand", just as if we were having an ordinary conversation, I asked again if this was ok. "Yes", she said, "that is fine", and I proceeded to ask her the following questions: "Do you believe in God?". "Yes, I do". "Do you believe that Jesus, his only son, God in the flesh died on the cross for you and was raised from the dead?" "Yes, I do". "Are you sorry for all your sins, can you forgive anyone who has ever hurt you?". She hesitated. I can tell you a few seconds in a situation like this as you wait on the answer can seem like an hour, you can also feel that everyone is watching you. I stopped at this point for a second or two and asked Jesus in my spirit to help her. "I feel that you have a bit of unforgiveness in your heart for someone," I said. She agreed that she had. I asked her if she could now forgive them. She pondered a while: "I mean from your head to your heart, not the pump in your chest nor from your head to your mouth". She looked at me and said "I am not sure I can do this". I said: "okay, I will ask the Lord to help you", and I said a little prayer asking that in the name of Jesus and by the power of His

Holy Spirit she would be set free of unforgiveness. I then asked her again and she replied: "Yes, I can do this", so we continued with the prayer: "Lord, help me to forgive all those who have hurt me, I ask forgiveness from all I have hurt. Lord, you are greater than the spirit of emotions, and I ask you to bind that spirit of fear in me and release me from it. Father I ask for the gift of your Holy Spirit. I receive the Holy Spirit as I repent for my sins: fill the cavity of loneliness within me with your Holy Spirit; fill me with that peace that defies all human understanding, increase my measure of faith in you; Lord, fill me from head to toe and from finger tip to finger tip with your Holy Spirit. Your Son is the light of the world, and the darkness that I have been in cannot hide his light. Thank you Lord; thank you Jesus; praised and glorified be your name". At this point I addressed the question about her husband coming back from the dead. "Now", I said, since you have invited Jesus into your life, through revelation, you will understand why your husband will not come back and tell you where he is. "Do you recall from your school days the Bible story about Lazarus and the rich man?" I asked (Luke 16/19-31) and I quoted: "There was once a rich man who dressed in the most expensive clothes and lived in great luxury every day. There was also a poor man named Lazarus, covered with sores, who was brought to the rich man's door, hoping to eat the bits of food that fell from the rich man's table. Even the dogs would come and lick his sores. The poor man died and was carried by the angels to the bosom of Abraham. The rich man died and was buried, and in Hades, where he was in great pain, he looked up and saw Abraham, far away, with Lazarus at his side. So he called out, "Father Abraham! Take pity on me, and send Lazarus to dip his finger in some water and cool my tongue, because I am in great pain in this fire!" But Abraham said, "Remember, my son, that in your lifetime you were given all the good things, while Lazarus got all the bad things. But now he is

enjoying himself here, while you are in pain.
Besides all that, there is a deep pit lying between us,
so that those who want to cross over from here to
you cannot do so, nor can anyone cross over to us
from where you are". The rich man said, "Then I beg
you, father Abraham, send Lazarus to my father's
house, where I have brothers. Let him go and warn
them so that they, at least, will not come to this place
of pain". Abraham said, "Your brothers have Moses
and the prophets ? with the word of God to warn
them; your brothers should listen to what they say".
The rich man answered, "That is not enough, father
Abraham! But if someone were to rise from death
and go to them, then they would turn from their
sins". But Abraham said, "If they will not listen to
Moses and the prophets, they will not be convinced
even if someone were to rise from death". Apply
what Jesus said in that story to the question about

your husband coming back to tell you where he is. I believe that the physical body of the rich man died and turned to dust. His spirit body was in Hades, the abode of the dead – a place of eternal punishment. You cannot harm a ghost or spirit. His spirit body knew that he was thirsty, he could see, he could hear, he could feel, reason and think. If you cannot hurt a ghost or spirit, the rich man could not have been in physical pain, I believe his spirit body, that has a soul was in emotional pain. Scripture says, that there is conscious existence after death.

John, she said, "I understand now what the scripture means, it has to do with faith, thank you". As I got into my car, she came running back and said to me: "I feel great, and I am glad I met you today". I said "I was glad to be able to share the good news with you". Dolores heard every word, were it not that she did, I doubt if she would have believed the story.

This

choice therapy

that I know works, is built on truth.
The living Word of God and not
on pious opinions.

The Word is timeless.

You believe by the power of the

Holy Spirit or you don't as the

true testimonies prove

If you think you have problems, read

Paul

and

Catherine's Testimony

as written by themselves that covers death, drug abuse, unforgiveness, loneliness and guilt.

By invitation, I John Manning, knocked on the door of Paul and Catherine's house, while Jesus was knocking on the door of their hearts.

Meet them now in their testimony.

When God healed - there was no withdrawal

My name is Paul, I am thirty eight. My wife's name is Catherine, she is thirty three. We came to know

Jesus Christ, in a personal way six years ago. I was baptised into the Roman catholic church as an infant and practised as a Roman catholic most of my life. As I reached the age of seventeen I lapsed and did not practice any religion, until I was twenty five. I had a personal crisis when I broke up in a relationship with a girlfriend that I was living with.

There is nothing more important than a fix !

I was taking a lot of drugs at the time and the hopelessness of everything took its toll. I gave God an ultimatum. It went something like this; if He made my life worth living again, I would believe in Him and start going to mass again. To me in my selfishness, it seemed like God was getting a real bargain. Although I practised my religion, I was an empty shell. I still lived life the way I wanted, I suited myself to a greater or lesser degree. I had a very slavish nature and sought pleasure and followed the path of least resistance.

When I met Catherine my priority at that time was to become a parent, to father a child. A caring and loving relationship was not a priority. So you can imagine the memory bank and the selfish sinful nature I was operating out of.

Was God getting his own back, because our babies were born out of marriage ?

Our first two children were born out of marriage, so you can see what my faith level was like, religion or no religion. Our third child, Ashlin, was born on Ash Wednesday, hence her name. She was a puny, delicate child. A couple of weeks later we took her out to a St Patrick's Day Parade. In Ireland we have a tradition of picking a cold, windy or wet day for this event. Within eighteen hours she was hospitalised with double pneumonia, and they transferred her to the National Children's Hospital. It was suspected that she had a heart condition. They carried out various tests and discovered a large hole in her heart along with several other defects. The medical team assured us that some of the defects were correctable, but the infections on the lungs had to be cleared up first.

We found the waiting and wondering, really hard. A couple of weeks later they carried out surgery. There was no real improvement, so they decided on more surgery. The result of all these operations was negligible. As the weeks wore on, Ashlin was still in intensive one to one care, on a ventilator, being drip fed with plasma and a variety of heart drugs. She was also being fed by tube. A few months later things were more or less the same, the doctor said that the situation was comparable to an eleven stone man dropping his weight to five stone through illness, and then having to run a twenty six mile Marathon. He posed the question to us "did you think the man could complete the distance?" of course not was our answer. "Well", he said, "the odds are twenty to one that Ashlin will breathe again in her own strength" This mind shattering news, was the most tragic situation we had ever faced. We could do absolutely nothing about it. We would have changed places with Ashlin but that was not possible. We were trapped and helpless. It had been in the hands of nurses, doctors and surgeons and all the technology but nothing had really happened, she was still as sick as ever. My mother asked an evangelist named John Manning, who has a healing ministry to come and pray with us. He refused saying we would have to invite him, not the granny, as Ashlin was our child and he did not interfere in people's lives, but would come and talk with us if invited.

He arrived one night as arranged, we were broken hearted, in bits. We heard the knock on the door, opened it and invited him in. He sat down with us and explained by way of his testimony, why he was doing what he was doing. "How, when his wife was crippled with arthritis and he himself was in financial dire straits had someone pray with him at a Christian Convention. He outlined what the life changing result of that prayer was when he received God's peace and conversion. We held hands and as we sat around the table and confessed ourselves as sinners, John led us in the following prayer that the Lord had given him".

The healing and conversion prayer.

"Father in Heaven, you created my innermost being, you knit me together in my mother's womb. I praise you because I am fearfully and wonderfully made, your works are wonderful, I know full well. I am suffering right now as you know. I repent for all my sins and ask your forgiveness, through your son Jesus, whom I accept as my Lord and Saviour. By the power of you Holy Spirit, make me the person that you want me to be, and not the person that I want to be. I accept that your son Jesus died on the cross for my sins and sicknesses and in His name and by the power of your Holy Spirit ask you to be with us now. Lord, help me to forgive all who have hurt me – and send your Holy Spirit to those I have hurt, so as that they can forgive me. I know that repentance makes prayer worthy. I now claim the gift of the Holy Spirit, the first of the gifts. Give me an extra measure of faith, wisdom and discernment that I can apply to my every day life. Your Spirit within me is greater than the spirit of emotions that Catherine and I are experiencing now, like resentment, fear, anger, hate, pride, depression, loneliness, poor self image not letting go of children, bad memories etc. I am in darkness, Heavenly Father, I ask you in Jesus' name to set me free and heal Ashlin, fulfil the plan you have for us as a family.

"Then he asked us to do the hardest thing we had done in our lives and that was to thank God for the situation. Not because God caused it, but because he allowed it to happen. The second that this was said, we both started hyperventilating: we didn't know if the floor was disappearing underneath us, or if we were going to go through the ceiling. We both cried like children as the power of the Holy Spirit was released into our lives. John had watched my wife Catherine's breathing pattern, which was nearer to hyperventilation than proper breathing. He said that these were rejections that she had experienced during her life. The last breath was the biggest and loudest.

loudest. Catherine felt immediately that was the rejection that she had received from her mother.

All these burdens were lifted and a peace descended on us that made our intolerable lives tolerable. The little finger of God's right hand really touched us in a big way. John blessed us with olive oil. He said no cloth or substance can hold a blessing. In my ignorance I proceeded to question him about who had blessed the oil and how holy it actually was. John explained, little did I know at the time that all blessings come from God and the blessing depends on your level of faith and of the person praying with you. Obedience to the Word makes the oil holy. Jesus says lay your hands on the sick.

He blessed our hands and amidst the tears and peace we drove over to the hospital to Ashlin at eleven thirty p.m. bringing the Christ who was now alive within us, the one with whom we now had a one to one relationship. The three of us went into the ICU and laid hands on Ashlin. We could feel a definite presence of the Lord in and around the cot as we prayed. What a joy to know that the situation was not ours any more. The burden of the last few months and years had been removed".

Strange Happenings

That night we were full of joy at our new found strength and peace. We slept decently for the first time since Ashlin was hospitalised. At about 4.00 am, I awoke and felt a sensation of what can only be described as pins and needles in one of my legs. As time passed the sensation increased and extended up and down the full extent of my body. The words that came to mind and later to my lips were "Lord, make me an instrument of Thy peace, make me an instrument of Thy love". At this stage Catherine was awake and sitting upright in the bed staring at me in disbelief. Tears welled up and were streaming down my face. She said she could actually feel the energy of electricity for want of a better word that washed over me. This lasted for about twenty minutes. With difficulty we went back to sleep wondering what was going on. John had said that we needed a living faith, from minute to minute, hour to hour, day to day, week to week, month to month and year to year.

You need a living faith, second to second, hour to hour, day to day, week to week, month to month, year to year.

The next day came and we had our usual visit to the hospital. All through the day I thought about what had happened. The question kept coming up about where children go when they die. Sure I had learned in church and school, that we went to heaven if were good and hell if we were bad. But where was this place Heaven? Was Ashlin going to go there for sure?. That night I wondered about our bodies being the temporary earthly dwelling places of the Holy Spirit. And the fact that we only have the loan of each other and that God has fixed the time allotted for each one of us. John had said the night before, that when children die they go directly to Heaven, having not reached the age of reason, they have no conscious sin and are blameless in the sight of God. As I got to bed that night and my head hit the pillow, I looked up toward the ceiling and there appeared a perfect triangle, whose edges were of white light. I rose up into the triangle and found myself in what seemed to be space or some kind of translucent blackness and it was raining. But no ordinary rain, small flakes of red, blue and gold rained down. Instantly, I was back in this vision or whatever, it was a glimpse into the heavens and lasted no longer than a minute or two. You can imagine Catherine's awe when I told her what had happened. The next day we went over to see Ashlin, there was no real improvement. We prayed and took out a bible, which we kept under her cot. Between the pages we kept a print out of an embryo scan, which Catherine had done when she was pregnant at the six month stage, to our amazement a big blotch of white light appeared in the centre of the photocopy. It had been in a plastic folder and could not have been contaminated or interfered with to produce such an effect. We rang John Manning and told him some strange and unusual things had been happening. Could we meet up and talk them over with him? He arrived at the hospital with his friend Liam where we recounted the things of the night before the electrical bath at bedtime, the triangle and the light patch on the photocopy. The first thing, John and Liam said was "Look", you have been blessed. What happened was you received the baptism of the Holy Spirit and the signs and wonders to go with it, but you will only know for sure when you see your life has changed. If your life and attitude has changed, I have read since that old men will dream dreams, and young men will see visions. You have had a conversion experience. Now what you must do is make Jesus, Lord and Master of your life and hand your problems or desire for Ashlin to be healed over to Him.

Her condition worsened and she was downgraded

Ashlin was going through a bad time, her lungs were still infected and it was imperative that they get her breathing by herself. At this stage she was six months on the ventilator. The longer this went on the less chance she would have of breathing independently. She was moved from the intensive care unit and down graded to a Special Care ward. Her condition had worsened and they could not afford any more time or space in intensive care. As a desperate and last ditch measure, they took her off the ventilator to see if she could manage to breath by herself. Two days later a doctor told us she was dying, her heart was beating at two hundred and twenty beats per minute, seventy was the norm. They asked us if we would like her confirmed and we said yes. A priest arrived and proceeded to carry out the sacrament. He was oblivious to the fact that as the blessing was taking place all the life-support machines went on the blink. You could cut the air, it was that intense with the presence of the Holy Spirit. Instantaneously, when the nurses adjusted the monitors the heart beat rate read a steady seventy beats per minute, down from the frantic two hundred and twenty. Ashlin slept peacefully all that night.

The next day her heart rate started to increase again. Discreetly the staff gave us brochures on how to make arrangements for a child's burial. They asked us if we would like to put her in a Moses basket, they used this basket to let the children die in the privacy of the bereavement room. We declined the offer. One progressive nurse asked us if we would like to take Ashlin home, so that she could pass on in more convivial circumstances.

They took her out of the main Special Care ward and put her down at the end of the corridor in a cubicle of her own where they stored hospital equipment. It was quite dirty, but it took me three days to realise it, because I was so intently watching Ashlin to see if she was breathing.

At this stage they stopped her medication and a day or two later her peripheral lines closed down, i.e. all the veins where they could insert their needles. They could not continue to give morphine. The chief anaesthetist gave us some words of consolation.

"Most people", he said, "have the idea that you go to hospital when you are sick and leave when you are well, but you may not. He admitted we were in a difficult position but so were the hospital and the medical experts. What we needed was a miracle as the doctors had given up except for one who said "When there is nothing else, there are always miracles". God was having the last word. This went on for ten days. Teams of people were praying intercessary prayers and this is also a testimony to the power of prayer, and the fact that God cannot refuse a humble and a contrite heart.

The response to the treatment was good.

Eventually the consultant's assistant peeked his head around the door and said that they were going to start medical treatment again. Ashlin began to respond slowly but surely. She cleared her infections and began to gain weight. The faith of the people anticipating a miracle was tested like gold in the fire. It took another three months before Ashlin was released from hospital. They told us she would be on heart drugs for the rest of her life. One year later she was hospitalised for measles. The first thing they did was take her off her heart drugs. When she was three she went for her half-yearly check up. The consultant remarked on her progress. One month later she got her feeding tube removed. Her heart is still very defective and they plan a heart operation between the age of three and ten. She has a good quality of life and we know that we only have the loan of her. The Lord has blessed us with a peace – the real miracle about the whole situation is we know we have a mighty God on our side who stands by us in all circumstances. We know now, Our God can use the most awful and hopeless situations in which to express and let us know of his unconditional love.

God took away my desire for drugs and there was no withdrawal.

I was a drug addict from the age of seventeen years. John told us about Dolores' miracle. In my brokenness through the sickness of my child God took my desire for drugs away and put in its place a pearl of great price. I was looking for physical healing for my daughter.

John did not know about my drug addiction when he came to pray with us, but the Lord wanted to heal me spiritually. I did not think I had any problems outside of my sick daughter. I had a sick spirit and a lot of sick emotions, which led to wrong values and morals. The root cause of this as John explained was my Adam and Eve nature. I would be copping out if I did not take responsibility for the things I have done and said, and the things I haven't done and said. I now know from my new found knowledge of the Word of God, I needed a Saviour to pull me out of the sorry state I was in and I needed the Holy Spirit to lead me and help me to rise above the pitfalls of life, that is why John asked, if I would like to ask for the gift of the Holy Spirit. He called it a "Forgotten Power" – that helps us cope.

Continuing on with my testimony even though five years have passed. I would have to say in retrospect that the peace Catherine and I received on the night that we invited Jesus into our lives has never left us. Jesus has always been faithful, and has given us unaccountable grace and blessings over the last years. He says in (Joel 2.25) "So I will restore to you the years that the swarming locust has eaten". Imagine I now can quote and understand the word of God.

We would have to confirm that as a family, God's redemption plan has been fully implemented in our lives. The walk of faith is a minute by minute, hour by hour endeavour, but Jesus never lets you down.

As I mentioned in the last section of my testimony, our daughter, Ashlin, began a slow and steady recovery. The next year was very demanding on us as we had quite a lot of work giving Ashlin all the time and things she needed to have a reasonable quality of life. After the second year she was medication-free and able to feed in her own strength. She was developing normally for someone with all the heart problems that she had. The Lord blessed us with another child, named Rebecca, and this helped Ashlin enormously, as there was just one year between them and as they grew, they became great friends and tried out many manoeuvres together. Our priorities as adults and parents changed.

As a family unit we bonded together with the cement of the Holy Spirit. Gone were most of the deep seated resentments, hurts and the anger which went along with them as we let God work out His Plan for us from which came the peace, joy, patience, self-control and the fruits of the Holy Spirit that go along with it. We still had problems - employment, housing, day to day decisions that had to be faced but with Jesus in our lives, we were never alone and even if we slipped and fell, we knew He was ultimately in control.

A strong interest began to grow within us for God's Word. Both Catherine and myself were continually amazed with the Scripture as we read day by day and got nourishment from things in His Word and the profound truth of it. Along with John Manning, the man who initially prayed with us, we became involved in a prayer group in which I had a music ministry. It was a real time of growth, we know now we were babes on spiritual milk, full of enthusiasm. We often got ourselves into hot water trying to explain this new found wealth. As the opportunities arose we got involved with John Manning in outreach work, any place where we could get a platform, we spoke at Full Gospel Business Men's venues, prayer meetings, conventions, seminars, even schools wherever we could lift up the Name of Jesus, who said "If I be lifted up from the earth, I will draw all men unto Me".

We were also getting into the one to one situations which were great for learning how the Holy Spirit works and casting light on the various areas that the Lord wants to deal with in a person's life. We learned the importance of praying God's plan into a situation and not our own agenda. It is easy for the ego to enter into a situation and man's pride to take over. We thinking we have something to offer or give when in our heart of hearts we know, as it says in (James 1/17) "Every good and every perfect gift comes down from the Father of Lights with whom there is no variation or shadow of turning".

I had been working on and off over the last ten years in the arts, mostly three-dimensional projects, sculpture etc. Slowly over the last five years since I came to know the Lord, a more Christian influence has emerged in the work. I would attribute this to the transforming power of God's Word. I would see the work not just as art but as objects of evangelisation helping the viewer to find parallels in the symbolism and imagery of the pieces joining to their situations. The pieces are useful in helping one grow in the revelation and wonder of God's creation.

"We are glad

John knocked on our door".

Now

Paul and I Catherine are knocking

on YOUR door,

IF YOU CANNOT COPE.

*

We now know what John meant
by the forgotten power like him,
we have experienced it.

As one of the church leaders said recently "The task of evangelisation of our young people is one of the most urgent priorities facing us, as we prepare for the year 2000. In a society which is becoming more individualistic and selfish, it is essential that as a Christian community, we give our young people a chance to know Jesus Christ and His gospel.

I find this a challenging task living in this day and age, the most precious gift which was given to me was the knowledge of the unconditional love of Jesus Christ. Now in turn I think it is the most important and essential message we can give to anyone, by helping them through the decision making process:

(1) Repentance (2) Forgiveness (3) Adult conversion to the person of Jesus Christ (4) Baptism in the Holy Spirit (5) Water baptism by immersion.

When the Holy Spirit comes into your life a great change takes place, the peace is permanent and He does a good job, which religion, ritual, or set of rules cannot achieve, i.e. make us worthy of the promises of Christ as revealed in His Living Word.

Ashlin was still being checked every six months to see how her development was going. They had already told us that at some stage they were considering a major operation. When Ashlin was four, they took her in to do extensive tests. The outcome of these was that one lung was damaged beyond repair from all the infections she had when she was first hospitalised. The other lung was in good condition but the blood supply was very poor. As she grew in size and stature it became harder and more physically demanding for her to walk long distances, run for a period etc.

The surgeon called us in one day and told us the situation and asked us to consider the option of open heart surgery. This would increase the blood supply to the good lung. As usual there were certain risks attached to the operation. The surgeon said that the failure rate was one in three. As the man pointed out that since there were three people in the room, himself, Catherine and myself, if the three of us were to undergo the surgery one of us would die. It brought home to us the seriousness of the situation. We felt our hearts sink as we left his office. We thanked the Lord for allowing all this to happen, and for knowing that whatever we had to go through, He was going to be there with and for us. As the day wore on I felt my peace was being robbed as I thought about the day's events and what the worst case scenario could be. Catherine and I talked and brought the whole situation before the Lord in prayer. He spoke His reply and in a quiet reassuring voice. I heard the words and I quote the following:

"Ashlin is My child
I have put My mark on her
I will not take My hand off her
Until My plan is complete"

What a reassurance this was in a time of uncertainty. As we looked up all the key words in the Bible for the answer to our prayer CHILD, MARK, HAND, PLAN AND COMPLETE, the peace returned as we got confirmation of all the good and perfect things He wants for us, as we left it in His hands. This was May 1996.

The hospital planned the operation for the summer of that year. Catherine was expecting again and the new baby was due in November. A hot summer would have done wonders for a child recuperating from major surgery. As the days-weeks passed the operation was postponed three times. Eventually it was confirmed for September, but depending on emergencies it could be postponed at the last moment. The time arrived for Ashlin to be admitted so she could undergo the pre-operation tests and treatment. She ended up in isolation as they thought she might have bacteria so they kept her quarantined. I spent every waking moment with her. After three days they let her home for the weekend. She was in great spirits to be back with her sisters again. The operation was planned for the Monday. We checked in on the Sunday evening and as we settled in for the night, we had a visit from the Hospital Chaplain. I told him of the hope I had in God's plan and we prayed that only His plan be carried out. A few days previous we had a visit from the Cardiac Liaison Nurse who pointed out the seriousness of the situation and the possibility of Ashlin dying as a result of the operation. I did not want to think about that, my focus was wrong. It was as if I was admitting that the medical profession had the power to let live or let die, whereas my faith tells me as it says in (Revelation 1.18) "And I have the keys of Hades and of Death". Once I realised that a far Greater Power than anything human was in control, I was at peace.

We felt Ashlin was downgraded in terms of importance!

The staff nurse told me that Ashlin would be the last of the three heart operations they were going to carry out that day. This in itself was bad news as it meant she had been downgraded in terms of importance. As the morning wore on I kept Ashlin occupied with games and activities, she asked if she could get out of bed and get dressed. Eventually they arrived with the trolley and we went down to the Operating

Theatre. She began to get agitated and frightened. I took her favourite blanket and tucked her in and asked the Holy Spirit to comfort her so she would be calm. The tension was almost unbearable as they applied the sedation and she passed out. I prayed all the time that God would carry out His plan. I went home and it took me all my strength to focus on my Lord and Master, and praise and thank Him for allowing it all to happen. We rang the hospital on several occasions but they had no news as to how things were progressing. As it was a six hour operation we had plenty of time in which to return to the hospital. Ashlin was removed to the Intensive Care Unit, the surgeon had left word that the operation had been very difficult.

They switched off the life support machine

In all, we got into the ICU three times that night going into the following morning. Each time we prayed as we laid hands on our child that the Lord's plan would be carried out. Her condition deteriorated until they called us in and we switched off the life support system. We laid hands on Ashlin and thanked the Lord for the loan of her and for all the memories and graces which he gave us through her. We also asked forgiveness for all our faults and our failings as parents and we claimed that forgiveness in the Lord's name. We asked the Lord to take her and for the angels to accompany her to the bosom of Abraham.

Her physical life has ended and her spirit body a living soul has returned to God to live for ever.

We kissed and hugged her, and were overcome by grief at the loss of our child. Through the tears we prayed and the staff affirmed the prayer. When we said that she was now in a much better place, one of the surgeon's team said "that is for sure". Her death became a real witness for those on duty that night in the ICU. They had never heard anyone pray like that before or accept what had happened in such a manner. We were certainly not great but the Lord was and His Holy Spirit, the comforter, worked overtime with us helping us through the situation.

We drove home and arrived about three thirty a.m., my brother had been babysitting. We told him what had happened and relieved him of his duty. The next morning when the children awoke we took them into the bed beside us, Teresa eight, Lis five and Rebecca three, (who had been Ashlins' best friend,) and told them of the death of their sister, we all had a good cry. It is difficult for three and six year olds to understand death the way more grown up children and adults do. It is almost a novelty, as all the people gather around the bereaved family, the attention and social aspect of the situation often block out and temporarily sustain people and it is not until afterwards that feelings of loss are experienced.

Like Abraham, in faith we must be able to see beyond physical death.

Arrangements were made to have a funeral and cremation ceremony. Since her name was Ashlin and she was born on Ash Wednesday, we thought it fitting that she should be cremated. Since the Bible says that we are only Sojourners and Transients on this earth it is nice to have her ashes with us wherever we happen to be. We had a simple ceremony with spontaneous readings from the Scripture by those who felt led by the Spirit to read and share the significance of what the Living Word meant in the present circumstances.

At the Mass, Ashlin's God father, John Manning, said that we only have a loan of one another in this world. He spoke of how Abraham had entertained angels or messengers and how Abraham could look beyond the physical death of his son, had he his dad killed him. Abraham trusted in God to have a better plan for his son and drew the comparison of Ashlin being a messenger who caused the message of the Good News Conversion to take root in our lives. This was confirmed for me a few days later, when I got this word that God said that our need for salvation was greater than Ashlin's need for physical healing. God allowed all that happened to happen so that we could know He loved us so much that He sent his only Son to die on the cross for us. The funeral was a celebration of Ashlin's life, all the people touched by the struggle she had from the time she was born until the time when the Lord called her home, her purpose and his plan fulfilled.

We long to be where Ashlin is but we know the greatest gift God has given us after His unconditional love is the gift of time to spend with each other. We also know we have been given a challenging and radical message and the command to (Mark 16/15) "Go into all the world and preach the gospel to every creature".

We know that we have treasure in clay pots and blessings and abundance from our heavenly family for our earthly family, in all circumstances our needs are met. Our child is in Heaven totally healed and will be there to welcome us when we too are called home. We had to get together as a family every day for months to call on the Lord, the author and perfecter of our faith, to help us through the day to day heartfelt loss and hurt of our grief. It is now almost ten months since Ashlin went to be with the Lord. We recently went to a day seminar, which the hospital organised for parents who had suffered bereavement of a child. We were amazed with the questions and burdens that almost all of the parents were still carrying with them. Not being able to let go, not being able to believe where their children were. In some cases it was two or three years and the raw grief and emotion was still causing terrible pain.

Everyone has a need for Jesus in their lives, there is no pain, hurt, problem that He can't help you to rise above and overcome. So if you are reading this and you haven't already invited Jesus into your situation, go ahead and invite Him in, He stands at the door gently knocking. Lord Jesus Christ Your Word says: (1 John 1/8) - If we claim we have not sinned, we make him out to be a liar and his Word has no place in our lives.

OVER THE NEXT FEW PAGES CATHERINE CONFIRMS PAUL'S TESTIMONY.

I was expecting my third child at twenty nine years of age, I prayed to God in my stupidity not to be pregnant, and to help me win the Lotto if I was. My husband and I were constantly rowing, and into this horrible environment our daughter Ashlin was born, on Ash Wednesday.

At two weeks old she was rushed into hospital barely breathing. She had caught pneumonia and both her lungs were full of fluid. It was discovered from X-rays that she had major heart defects. Ashlin was put into an intensive care unit in the National Children's Hospital in Dublin. She was connected to a breathing machine (ventilator) which did all her breathing for her, a morphine drip was keeping her sedated while her heart was being monitored. The first thing you notice in the unit is that among all the babies there is no crying, the only sound comes from the bleeping of the machines. After two minor operations, five months later, the doctors lost hope for her, she was given one chance out of twenty of surviving independently without any assistance from the machines.

The black hole within me, was consuming me.

The surgeon, Mr Woods, said "for Ashlin to come off the breathing machine and to breathe by herself, was like an eleven stone man who dropped his weight to five stone through illness, and to get him to run a twenty six mile marathon, would be an impossibility". The nurses gave us great support but it was not enough. The black hole that was inside of me was consuming me. I was totally lost. I had figured in my mind that God was punishing me for not wanting the child, and for having two children outside of marriage. But I now know that God is a loving God as it says in 2 Peter 3 v 9.

The Lord is not slow in keeping His promises as some understand slowness. He is patient with you not wanting anyone to perish, but everyone to come to repentance.

My mother in law invited John Manning, a member of her prayer group to pray with us. We were so desperate at this stage that we agreed. Instead of turning up at the hospital, he came to our home. We sat at a table and John came to share with us about his life and how God brought him out of his darkness into the light. After we joined hands to pray, we thanked God for allowing Ashlin to be sick, for allowing her to be exactly as she was. This was a very difficult thing for me to say, but we both thanked God, and accepted that God allowed but did not cause it to happen.

(Rom. 8 v 28) We know that in all things that God works for, the good of those who love Him, who have been called according to His purpose. As we prayed for forgiveness for our sins and accepted Jesus into our lives we asked for the baptism of the Holy Spirit. John poured olive oil on my hand, God wanted me and Paul to be healed, we were sick in our hearts. (James 5 v.14) Asks is anyone of you sick ? "He should call the elders of the church to pray over him and anoint him with oil in the name of the Lord". Immediately I felt the Holy Spirit, flowing over me in waves of warmth, it lasted a few minutes, releasing me from all my worries bringing me out of darkness into the light. From that day on I have had a great peace, love and joy beyond human understanding. At midnight or thereabout, John, Paul and myself went to see Ashlin in the ICU and we prayed with her. Again I felt the presence of the Holy Spirit flowing into her, ministering to her we anointed her head with oil in the sign of the Cross.

When the Holy Spirit moves you know it.

You would think at this stage that she would be recovering, but she got a lot worse. The medical team turned off her oxygen slowly and switched her to an oxygen tent, after removing the ventilating tube from her breathing passage. After they did so Ashlin let out a little cry, it was a long time since we had heard her do this. Her heart was beating so fast at this stage it looked likely she would go into cardiac arrest, so she was confirmed. The nursing team prepared a room away from everyone else, so she could die in peace. Her morphine drip was removed as all her veins had collapsed. We had to watch very closely to see if she was breathing, as her tiny body was so weak and thin she hardly ever moved.

We had teams of people praying intercessory prayer for Ashlin here and in other countries, some were even fasting. Seven days had passed with all treatment stopped and she still lived. I remember one morning especially it was the day she came around, the nurses said "this was it", she was at death's door. But as we told her I talked to God and said "even now Lord, I believe" she opened her eyes and lived. The doctors were amazed, they came back and started treating her again. It was the tenth day, and Ashlin was getting stronger and stronger with each passing day. It was a long hard struggle that was only possible by knowing God. (Luke 13 v. 7) "For nothing is impossible for God".

Nothing is impossible for God

Four and a half years later, after a hospital check-up, we received the news from the surgeon that her lungs had not developed and she needed surgery straight away or she would die slowly. We brought this before the Lord and thanked Him for allowing it to happen and like Jesus in the Garden of Gethsemanie, we prayed for His will to be done, not ours. The operation was due in the summer of 1996, I was pregnant with my fifth child. We thought the earlier she had the operation the better chance she would have of surviving it. But thank God, he had better plans.

(Is. 55 v. 8-9)

"For my thoughts are not your thoughts, neither are your ways my ways" declares the Lord. As the heavens are higher than the earth so are My ways higher than your ways and My thoughts than your thoughts. The operation was put back three times until October the first. She had open heart surgery on that Monday morning, we were called in that night. We prayed with her in the ICU on the bed among all the machines while the team worked on the life support systems. We thanked God for the operation, we prayed for God's will to be done and we handed Ashlin over to him. Ashlin died that night, she left us to go to her heavenly home to be with God.

(Ecc. 12 / 7) "And the dust returns to the ground it came from, and the spirit returned to God who gave it".

We thanked God for the loan of Ashlin

Looking back we have discovered one of God's many reasons for putting back the operation was because God wanted us to have one last summer on earth with our precious daughter.

One month after her physical death, a beautiful baby girl was born to us, perfect in every way. In our humanness we miss Ashlin every day and no child could replace her, our greatest blessing is how God brought us to His Son Jesus. We have received so much peace, love and joy from God.

(Luke 6 /.38)

"Give and it will be given unto you, a good measure pressed down, shaken together and running over, will be poured into your lap". We share with everyone who God wants, how He brought us from the darkness into the light. Our lives have completely changed. We now know God's love. We look forward to the day that we will be with God and all our loved ones in Heaven.

(Ephesians 5 / 8)

"For you were once darkness, but now you are light in the Lord. Walk as children of the light".

Paul and Catherine.

Theresa, Liz, Becky, Rachel and baby Adam (Joshua)

THE 7 a.m. HITCH-HIKER

Since starting to work as an evangelist I have come to realise that what we regard as meeting people by chance is not really so; it is part of God's plan. Being in a particular place at a particular time can have consequences we would never have dreamed. Let me tell you about the hitch-hiker. I was leaving a large town in Ireland one morning on my way back to Dublin when I passed a hitch-hiker carrying a back-pack. I had gone a few hundred yards when a little voice (or thought as I call it) said: "Pick him up." Contrary to my practice of not picking up hitch-hikers, I braked, and reversed to where the man was. In order to get into my small car, (I had sold the Mercedes, it was a pride thing) this very tall man had to remove his haversack. He put it on the roof of the car; then took off his anorak, saying as he did so:

"Thank God". When we settled into the two and half hour drive to Dublin, I asked him why he had said "Thank God". He said he was tired because of a two hour walk and no breakfast and was glad of the lift. He was on a month's leave of absence, hiking around Ireland, visiting holy shrines, hoping to find peace within himself. Having asked the Lord to guide me, I was led to tell him how I found God's peace, which is my testimony, like I am supposed to do.

Come with me as I share!

As we drove along the road, he told me he was going through a bad time. I told him that I knew what bad times are and proceeded with my story that is recorded in this book. I asked him if he was a priest, he said he was and took time out to find God if he was there. "Was your vocation, your mam's, dad's or family ?" "I am not sure. I know I am not at peace". I said "here we are driving along early in the morning with jackdaws on the road, cattle and sheep in the fields, the sky and heavens above like a canopy over us, but God is not any of the things we see. However, since my experience, I believe in God the Father and his only son Jesus and by the power of the Holy Spirit I believe and see His glory all around me. My faith is a living Faith from day to day, a precious gift to be received".

Every unmarried human being, whether priest, pastor, pope, bishop, brother, dustbin man, civil servant or nun must practice chastity, no sex unless you are married. God loves us whether we keep His commands or not, however if you do not repent before you die, you go to hell ?

The conversation came around to celibacy and chastity, when I asked was he gay or did have gay feelings, he said no. Well then, are you the type that falls in love three times a day, no he says just once a week. Would you like to be married ? It took a while for him to respond, like about a half a mile, twenty telegraph poles. I suppose over the years I did have feelings for some women, not all John, but some over the years. Would you believe Simon, (not his real name) that I believe that more poor unfortunate nuns, brothers and priests, real caring lovely people, have gone to hell and will continue to do so in the future, because of the celibacy and chastity rule, imposed by man? Anyway, the average priest does not take the vow of chastity, (not to have genital sex). If he does he commits the sin of fornication like anyone else that is not married, it is a forgivable sin. However a priest becomes a fraud when he cheats. We agreed and he asked how to overcome the desires of the flesh, so I shared the following... (1) Do like I did, invite Jesus into your life and ask for the gift of the Holy Spirit, then you are ordained by God, and not by man, and you will overcome by the power of the Holy Spirit. (2) If not, get out, that is better than lose your body and soul to Satan. You will get great support from your friends, but very little from your family. You are their meal ticket to heaven and the pride of the family. I had forgotten that he mentioned he had no breakfast, so I apologised and stopped at a restaurant for breakfast and continued our chat after I had phoned home to cancel two business appointments-I was glad that I had a few pounds that day. I told him that there are no visible or physical signs that you have received the Holy Spirit after you ask for it, some people fall to the floor, when prayed over. He said that he heard of people being slain in the Spirit and was that the same thing. I said it does not mean you have received the Holy Spirit, even though it did happen to me. I only knew when my life changed. You would know by the fact that the desires of the flesh, (natural sexual urges) would become controllable for the sake of the kingdom of God. Don't give in, stay in, give it a try, God has a plan for you, let him fulfil it.

You certainly cannot go on the way you are, you could turn to sexual body abuse, drink too much, become obese, get into pornography, be very unhappy, and live in misery here and when you die. God loves you, Roman Catholic priest or not. Then he asked would I pray with him for the gift of the Holy Spirit. So out to the car for prayer. You can be ordained by man and not be ordained by God. He had a Pentecostal experience, he is happy and content the Lord touched him, like the Lord touched me, he has a great peace now and can cope. And what a day I had, the next morning I got a great order for my product that I did not solicit.

I believe there are some great men and women, nuns, priests, pastors in all churches who need our prayers and need to be encouraged. God knows the cheats.

This healing and conversion prayer

I wrote for people in bereavement,

caused by the death of a loved one,

or some one they did not love.

"Father in Heaven you have created my inmost being, you knit me together in my mother's womb. I praise you because I am fearfully and wonderfully made, your works are wonderful. I know that full well.

I am not so well just now because of the death of
………………? I repent for all my sins and ask
your forgiveness through your Son Jesus, whom I
accept as my Lord and Saviour. Help me to forgive
all those who have hurt me (mention name of
deceased if he/she had hurt you) and send your Holy
Spirit to those living that I have hurt, comfort them
so that they can forgive me. Jesus I know that
repentance makes prayer worthy.

Having repented, I now ask for and claim the gift of
your Holy Spirit and receive it, the first of the gifts.
Give me the gift of faith, wisdom and discernment
now, as I ask and receive, so that I can apply them to
my everyday life. Your spirit within me is greater
than the spirit of depression, loneliness, bad
memories of deceased (if applicable) or anyone else,
or anger towards you my heavenly Father. Do not let
me retain any sin of unforgiveness towards any

person, I ask you in Jesus name. I cannot cope with the loss of..............? I am in darkness. Jesus light up this darkness and set me free, so that you can fulfil the plan you have for me. I thank you for the loan of...................? Thank you, Jesus, I praise and glorify your name.

(Composed by John Manning while reading Psalm 139)

The

Pub Theologin

ASKED ME
IF I THOUGHT THAT EVE WAS HAVING SEX,
AND PRACTISING INCEST
WITH HER SONS,
AND DID I THINK THAT THIS WAS THE
WAY
GOD POPULATED THE WORLD?

One cold and wet windy morning, as I was on my
way to a meeting in Dublin, a man stopped me and

asked was I the guy doing the Scripture sharing in the local convent, and would I mind if he asked me a few questions. As I tightened my coat around me to keep out the breeze, and invited the man under the confined space of my umbrella to keep us dry, I was wondering what was coming next.

Was I going to be clobbered?

As he dragged on a cigarette, he went on to say that he and his mates meet in the local pub most days to discuss the problems of the world and offer solutions, and no one listens. We call ourselves "the pub theologians". In recent times the Adam and Eve situation came up for discussion, and seeing that Adam and Eve, our first parents, had two boys, we figure there had to be incest going on between the mam and the sons, so my mates asked me to ask you what you thought. Well, I said, they had three children, Cain, Abel and Seth. However, like yourself, I was not around then and you look younger than I do, so we do not really know. I cannot see God, our creator, who tells us, his creatures, that incest is wrong, and forbids us to practise it, would then turn around and allow it in any circumstances to accomplish his own ends. After all, He is God the creator of all things. As the conversation continued, I asked would he like to discuss with his mates the following: "Were Adam and Eve symbolic, did God create a whole race of people at the same time that he created Adam and Eve and pull them out to represent the human race" ? Adam and Eve were never babies, they did not wear nappies, did they have belly buttons.? Adam was created from clay and died at age 930. Eve was created from the flesh of Adam, I do not know how long she lived. If they were created adults, they were never fed from theirs mother's breast. The pub theologian was all excited about the questions I put to him and was looking forward to the crack when he would put the same questions to his mates in the pub, where they once again would try to unravel the mystery of life/death. We discussed all the sins he and his mates had committed over the years, like missing mass and the guilt that came with it, which caused them to believe that God did not love them any more and so lost interest in the church, but not in God. I explained that God loves him and his mates just as they are, no matter how awful they thought they were.

I also explained to him, before I gave him the repentance, healing and conversion prayer, that it was not a sin to miss mass on Sundays, it was an obligation not fulfilled. However, I reminded him again that repentance made his prayers heard and conversion possible. The bible, which is God the creator's manual, tells us how to live and bring up our children. We teach our children the rules of life, the rules of the sports they play and the rules of the road. We have forgotten to tell them about God's unconditional love and his rules on how to live, cope, survive and overcome, whether we are sick or healthy, and be fruitful and happy in this life and know the promises of the next. Did I sow a seed that day with the pub theologian ? ; did I water a seed that only God can make grow? ; I do not know. We shook hands and off he went knowing now that in Jesus' name all his sins were forgiven and that God's love is unconditional, and that the plans he has for his creatures, you and I, will be revealed in Jesus' name.

The testimonies recorded in this book are about ordinary people their biblical priesthood and sainthood experiences.

I read the following on page 244 in the Flannery edition of Vatican II, under the heading of the Church to-day and I quote "The layman should also know that it is generally the function of their well formed Christian conscience to see that the divine law is inscribed in the earthly city. From priests they may look for spiritual light and nourishment. Let the layman not imagine that his pastors are such experts that to every problem that arises, however complicated, they can readily give him a concrete solution, or even that which is their mission. Rather, enlightened by Christian wisdom and giving close attention to the teaching authority of the church, let the layman take on this role". I DID, WILL YOU?

Testimony of

Dolores Manning

I remember when John told a church full of people that I Dolores his wife, was not the most important person in his life.

"My name is Dolores Manning and John my husband has shared our testimony with you in the early pages of this book which includes my miracle healing, as hundreds can witness to in our parish of Drumcondra, Dublin 9. Ireland and in other countries".

There is no cure for Rheumatoid Arthritis.

"For twenty five years plus, well before John and I had our experience with the Lord. I Dolores was treated at Dr. Collins' clinic for Rheumatoid Arthritis sufferers, at Lucan, Co. Dublin, Ireland.

They told me that they would not be able to cure me but could improve the quality of my life". They did give me hope, and kept my condition under control with their special treatment. We remember Dr. Collins senior and his wife, Dr. Richard and Dr. Patrick who have gone to be with God, with love and affection for their caring attitude. We pray God's blessing on Dr. Maurice who runs the clinic now, his family and staff and say thank you. I remember the day that Dr. Maurice told me that I did not have to go for treatment anymore.

Nothing is impossible for God.

"There was another miracle to come a number of years down the road after my healing that only God knew about, that showed us why God healed me. If you want to join me as I share this journey you are very welcome. I will start with what John said at a prayer meeting one night where he was invited to talk. I was sitting in the middle of a few hundred people half way down the church and locked into the middle of a row. Only one or two people knew that I was John's wife. After all the singing was finished, John was introduced and gave his testimony, which included my healing. He told the stunned people that I was not the most important person in his life, and waited for the place to calm down, and the whispering to cease, the silence was something else and I was gob smacked". "He then introduced me and asked me to stand up as he explained what the Apostle Paul says in Romans 8/9 "In fact unless YOU possessed the Spirit of Christ you do not belong to Him.

The Spirit of God must live *IN* you! If not you live in darkness". We as a couple found this to be true and experienced it, we came from darkness into the light and could now cope. When you can love Jesus first and only Jesus, by the power of the Holy Spirit, you can then love yourself and others. Because Jesus was first in his life John could love me in my awful painful condition. After all these years, Jesus is still the most important person in Johns' life. I do not have a problem with that, as Jesus is the most important person in my life. John coped with his health, my health and his business problems by the power of the Holy Spirit so did I. John shared the following scripture with me, half way through my healing when we thought healing had stopped. (Luke 14/26 says) "If anyone comes to me without turning his back on his father and mother, his wife and children, his brothers and sisters, indeed his very self, he cannot be my follower".

God healed me, turned Johns' business and health around in order to help us both through a great miracle **to come.** So hang in there if you want and John, who took the 6 a.m. phone call will share with you.

AMANDA

ARRIVED INTO THIS WORLD ON THE 24th. OF NOVEMBER 1993.

The phone rang at six a.m. 24th. November 1993. The voice on the other end said "dad will you pray with me?" "Sure I will" I said recognising that it was my own daughter Brid, so I asked where she was and what was wrong. Dad I am in the Rotunda Hospital my baby girl was born a few hours ago and things do not look good as to whether she will live or not. Together, we prayed the conversion and healing prayer on the phone, and thanked God for the situation. We also thanked him for the gift of faith that allowed us pray together, and asked God in Jesus' name to send the Holy Spirit and Amanda's (as we know her by name now) guardian Angel to be with her at that time. Brid made an appointment for 11 a.m. in the intensive care unit of the Rotunda Hospital, Dublin for her and I to pray with baby Amanda who was critically ill. Baby Amanda as she was eventually christened was all tubed and wired up. We were given very little hope, you did not have to be told things were not good, it was obvious. Brid and I stood around the hot cot as we called it, and I asked my daughter Brid what she wanted to ask God for, she said "I would like my baby to know that I am her mammy".

The prayer that we said around the hot cot, went like this...

"Heavenly Father I thank you in Jesus' name for the loan of my daughter, you have known her before you put her together in my tummy, you know her by the name that her dad and I have not given her yet. You did not cause her to be unwell you have allowed it because you know best. In my brokenness I ask in Jesus' name as we gather around her cot, that you will fulfil the plan you have for her, her dad and me her mammy. The news is not good, we were told by the medical people not to hold much hope, however nothing is impossible for you my Heavenly Father as my dad and I seek your kingdom first. Bless the nurses and the doctors as we leave the ward now and leave my baby in your care".

I the grandad went home and phoned people all over the world for prayer, and Brid went back to her ward. I the grandad said to God that if he spared my grandchild for the mammy and daddy that I would look after her if I was needed to do so for as long as it took.

I went in almost every day for the best part of four months to the Rotunda ICU and eight months approximately to Temple Street ICU. I read the scriptures every day with her as I held her little hand praying that her mammy and daddy would be able to cope. I prayed with more people in both hospitals during that twelve month period it was just great, the conversions (the start of a miracle) that took place were fantastic. The nurses and parents of sick children in both hospitals loved to hear me pray and listen to the words that I would say. Quite a lot of people including the nurses told me that they had a spiritual awakening that stayed with them. The tests were endless, month after month, hospital after hospital. I prayed God's will be done before scans, x-rays etc. They all came back clear. Amanda was eight last birthday thank God. She cannot walk or talk, is tube fed, talks with her eyes, and has a marvellous personality. She is full of the Holy Spirit like her mam and can cope only by the grace of God. Amanda and her mam live with Dolores and me the grandad now.

Every day is a long day. Now you can see that God who lives out side of time knew what was ahead for us and made provision. He healed Dolores and me the grandad in his time so as that we would be able to help with Amanda. You need two people after her mam leaves for work, most days at five a.m. Amanda's physical movements are restricted, but her spirit body is perfect like all spirit bodies are, special needs or not. We are all made for the next world, the Spirit world and depending on where your spirit body goes after the flesh body dies, you either live in perfect peace in heaven or in hell to be tormented for ever. Amanda can now say "Jesus" and thank you. She is a living saint and we thank God for her, and the privilege of looking after her every day and for the grace to do what we do. Dolores and I have an open invitation from my brother Dennis and his wife Terry in Australia, my nephew Nial and cousin Stephen in New Zealand, from Dolores' brother Al, Mona, Tony, Aleta in California, from our daughter Anne and Christopher in New York State, from our daughter Amanda and Patrick in Kentucky, USA and from Mr. and Mrs. Chuck Williams in Orlando, Florida to play golf and spend time with them. In fact as it says in my testimony Mr. and Mrs. Williams were party to our conversion, and we thank the Lord for them. However looking after Amanda who is so special is our New Zealand, America and Australia. When she is older, God willing we will travel.

(1)

Cured of Mylocytic Lukemia

My name is Susie and I was diagnosed with acute Mylocytic Leukemia six days before Christmas in 1991 at the age of 25. The night before going into hospital my boyfriend proposed to me. We did not know for sure at that time what the future held for us. I was brought up in the Roman catholic church, as were the rest of my family and I attended mass every Sunday. It was not until I was sick that I realized how much faith I had in God. It is hard to remember a lot of what happened while I was sick. One call I do remember is the phone call from my mam and dad asking if their friend Mrs. Stosiek, could bring along an evangelist chap by the name of

John Manning from Dublin, Ireland who prays with people who are sick. I said yes. I was very sick and also very nervous. I believed in the power of prayer but I was not sure how to pray. I had nothing to be nervous about. As soon as I met John, I felt I had known him for a long time. My then boy friend Russell, who is now my husband was present in the ward with us, and was not sure what to do or say. Before we started to say the healing prayer with Mrs. Stosiek, John told Russell not to join us as we prayed, unless the Lord grabbed him by the scruff of the neck and told him to join us, which he did. John wrote down the words we prayed on a scrappy piece of paper which I still have. It has always been tucked away in the pages of my Bible and once in a while I say the same prayer in thanks, for the extra years God has given me and the fact that I feel so good ten years later. Many things sustained me through that time-the great medical care from Doctors,' Nurses and staff. My sister Linda who was my bone marrow donor, she was so brave and I thank her. The love of family and friends, but most of all because I now know that God who loves me as he does all human beings healed me through praying His Word. I share the good news with you the reader like John did with Mrs. Stosiek, Russell and me Susie. God fulfilled His plan for all present that day and will for you also, if you ask in Jesus' name. Imagine travelling such a distance to pray with someone. John evangelized Russell and me, now we can evangelize others. John reminded me that he did not know me all his life, but as he and Mrs. Stosiek laid hands on me, the Word of God and

His promises that were in my heart for so long, were released by the power of the Holy Spirit, he and Mrs. Stosiek were the jump leads.

Russell and me Susie

(2)

She should be belly up in the canal behind Croke Park ?

Having had my experience, I brought empty jars before the Lord like Una, the woman at the Post Office, my mam and dad, Paul, Catherine and others. Una who should be belly up in the canal, her husband had done a runner with another women, her brother and his pals were starting on drugs, the scandal of it all would have killed her mam and dad and she herself was going nowhere, unable to cope. We prayed about it, Una herself gave her life to the Lord. God heard her request, heard her prayer, as repentance makes prayer worthy, and the lads stayed off the drugs. Una has a very good responsible job now, with excellent prospects, her own new car and house.

(3)

She was ready to jump !

Anne who was suicidal (I had spoken with her on the phone a few times the previous week and she was not great) was sitting on a window sill, ready to jump from four floors up. I was just making myself comfortable at home to watch one of the Irish international matches, when a thought came to me that I should phone this person, which I did; the jump never took place. God interrupted her life, she is great now and I missed the match, so what of it, it is God's time anyway. Anne has three lovely boys she reared herself with no help from the dad. She has a relationship with Jesus now and life is worth living. She also has a car and her own house.

(4)

The flash backs were awful ?

Kay phoned and through the tears said that she had had an *abortion.* I said the abortion forgiveness and conversion prayer with her, that you will find on page 378/379 in the question and answer section. She is married now and doing great, there is joy in her life again, no guilt and knows that the spirit body and soul of the baby she aborted has returned to God to be fulfilled as God had planned for the next life. She aborted the plan God had for her baby in this world, a forgivable sin. No more guilt or flash backs since.

(5)

Dad always told me and my sisters, that we were ugly!

Sarah who was sick on and off for twenty years, was emotionally scarred. She thought she was ugly and that no one cared. Her dad and mam it seemed to her never cared, which was borne out by their attitude. Sarah had terrible memories of her dad coming home drunk and beating mam, herself and her sisters telling them and Sarah the youngest in particular that they were all ugly. Healing has taken place, it took nine months and God's peace reigns in Sarah's heart.

(6)

The bad thief, he was always getting caught ?

The Beggar Man, was also a bad thief, who had more breakfasts in jail than anywhere else, for things he did not do. I met him one day, and as I gave him some money, I asked him why he was so unhappy? he said "if no one loved you, would you be happy"? After a thirty minute chat, I prayed the healing and conversion prayer with him on a street in Cork. He is not depressed anymore and knows that God loves him, knows him by his name not as a thief or beggar man. He often begs in Dublin for a change of scenery, and when he is in Dublin I usually meet him as I know where he will be.

(7)

Can you pray for animals to be healed ?

Margaret phoned from England and asked would I pray with her and, I said yes. Through the tears I discovered that she wanted me to pray for her sick dog that was diagnosed as having cancer and would die within four weeks, according to her "vet". I lead her in the healing and conversion prayer to discover that the real problem was that her husband did not love her any more, she had no children, all her love was showered on the dog. Never will she be so bad again, she now knows about God's unconditional love for her and her husband. She received the Holy

Spirit, her live has turned around, now she can love herself her husband and others. The relationship with her husband is great. I got her to say a prayer over the dog, the dog survived and was healed.

(8)

Blind

(unsighted)

but can see?

My friend David McKee is unsighted, he was not always like that. He lost his sight in both eyes over a number of years. He played football before he lost his sight and still loves to talk football even though he cannot see. He loves to listen to the matches on radio or television. He was angry with God for years, he is a very clever handsome chap and now works the special telephone switch-board, for a company in

Shannon that is very good to him, and he is good at his job.

He often says to me how great it is, that he and I can share scripture on the telephone with one another, talk about Gods' provision and share the good news. with one another. We are not spiritually deaf or blind like we were, even though he is physically blind, he can cope by the grace of God. He was baptised in the Holy Spirit a few years ago, and now knows that when his flesh body which is mortal dies, he will see Jesus with the eyes of his spirit body, as Jesus is. He knows that we are made for the next life and that things are not always as we want in this one. God is using him in a big way to help others. He is at peace with himself and God. He also knows that it is better to come into this world minus a leg, arm or eye, and not be able to see, than to lose his spirit body and soul to Satan when he physically dies, because of anger or resentment. He does get fed up with people saying it is God's will that he is blind. God did not cause his blindness, He allowed it, so when we call out to God in our brokenness in Jesus' name, God hears us and then we can cope, just like Job did.

(9)

They missed the plane to Australia so they thought.

My brother Dennis, his wife Terry and daughters Denise and Louise left Dublin for London a few years ago on their way to Australia. Dolores and I, plus our five children had lived in Los Angeles for five years. So we suggested that they should get off the flight in Los Angeles and visit Disneyland. To cut the long story short. They went to Disneyland and had a great time and got back to the airport in Los Angeles to be told that if they looked out the windows, they would see their plane just taking off. You mean we missed it "they asked", yes you did, they were told.

They hung around for quite a while in consultation with the staff of the particular airline and then left to stay in a hotel for the night at their own expense. They were waiting on a taxi or cab, when an airline official came running up and said "your prayers were answered, the plane is turning back, it burst a tyre taking off, so now you can we get you on board". I had prayed and told the chap who was my brother my testimony before he left, and how great God was and what he was doing in my life. They did get on the flight and arrived in Australia ok. Nothing is impossible for God.

(10)

It is one o'clock p.m. My friend and business associate is late for our lunch date in the Gresham Hotel in Dublin, real posh, and us with not a bean between us.

He eventually arrives all hot and bothered a little bit more than usual. This is the story, John he says "I am in fierce trouble to day". Tell me I said "what is" wrong? The bank manager won't pay a letter of credit for eighty thousand pounds Irish due to my main suppliers since yesterday. If I don't lodge eighty thousand pounds Irish before three o'clock today, I will be out of business. I had lunch and he had indigestion. We prayed the healing and conversion prayer. We asked in Jesus' name that the Holy Spirit would touch the bank managers' heart and that he would hold the letter of credit if we asked, by rebuking any spirit of the flesh in the bank managers' heart, that would cause him to refuse to pay the letter of credit. We phoned from the hotel, and got the manager of the bank, my friend told him that there was no way he would have the money before Friday. The bank manager asked him if he would definitely have the money for Friday, I am sure I will he replied. He did have the money before Friday, praise the Lord. Another request answered.

(11)

It happened in the Bon's Hospital, Glasnevin, Dublin 11.

I went to visit a friend who was having tests in the above hospital. She was afraid of what they might find. She was feeling lonely and sad, as it was not long since her husband had died. After a brief chat we got down to prayer, in fact now, that I can recall, I was a patient myself that week, and just went down to her ward for prayer and a chat. All of the other ladies in the ward wanted to join in and listen. This was agreed by my friend, they were all in the same boat lonely and afraid. As I sat on the edge of the bed of my friend Anne, holding hands with the other ladies in the ward, saying the healing and conversion prayer as a group, I noticed a lady come in and stand behind the door and join in the prayers. Now there were five ladies in the room. Eventually all went back to bed, I went back up to my ward, and the lady that came in last went to her ward further down the corridor. The next afternoon a lady came to my ward asking for me, John Manning, "I said I am he". I pulled a chair over and invited her to sit down. The three other patients in my ward all men of course, one of whom I often played golf with, were wondering who this glamorous woman was.

Having sat down she said in a whisper, "I followed you in that prayer you said with those ladies yesterday. I was a very disturbed lady and gave them a lot of hassle here in this hospital. In the prayer you covered a lot of things, however you seemed to be speaking to me particularly in the area of unforgiveness. Before I got back to my room a great peace came over me, to such a degree that I did not need medication to quieten me down or help me sleep that night. I am on my way home now, the doctor cannot imagine the change in me over night. Could I please have a copy of the prayer you said with us all yesterday. I would like to give you an offering". I said "thank you, but I do not take money". Off she-went Jesus set her free.

(12)

The oxygen mask !

On my way to visit my daughters in America, to do business, and some Evangelist's work, I felt as snug as a bug in a rug, as we set off over the Atlantic, thirty thousand feet nearer heaven. Note, I did not say nearer to God. The intercom came on and the Air Hostess addressed the passengers saying "if the oxygen mask falls down in front of you, put it on yourself first, then on others". It is the same in my business as an evangelist, if I am not evangelised I cannot evangelise others. If I keep preaching and do not spend time with the Lord, I may evangelise others and lose my own spirit body and soul. I must set aside time for the Lord.

(13)

People often say marriages are made in heaven ?

Someone said to a man who phoned me last year that marriages are made in heaven. This man's wife had done a runner. He replied by saying that this was pure rubbish. A lot of marriages in this country, like his own marriage, were / are made in hell. He believes that the concept of marriage was made in heaven and that is where it ends. He was baptised in the Holy Spirit and can now cope and is happy.

(14)

Could you have coped with the following?

I met my friend Sean Reilly at a conference some years ago, and travelled home with him on the ferry from England. On the journey to the ferry and on the ferry, we discussed our upbringing in relation to God religion and church. I shared with Sean what Jesus did for me by way of testimony. Just like myself he attended to his religious duties, taught his children the difference between right and wrong, and attended church out of duty to his family. Once Sunday mass was over he went about his business and nursing a sore head from drinking too many pints the night before, he would then get all the Sunday papers and read about every scandal in England and Ireland and rarely think of God. The story continues and Sean shares the following in love.

My life changed in September 1988. My wife Kitty had a growth in her throat and was losing her voice. The doctor said that she needed an operation, and the first thing that came to my mind was that she had cancer, the thought sent shivers down my spine. The thought of Kitty dying frightened me, our youngest daughter Lisa was eleven and Sean our son was five and like Lisa loved mammy very much. As Kitty packed her bag to go to Waterford Regional Hospital, I said for the first time in my life a prayer from my heart that changed my whole life and it went like this. " Lord God, I need Kitty here at home, I cannot manage on my own. I ask you to protect her and bring her home safe, thank you Lord." Kitty had a very successful operation and was home after five days. Soon after I was promoted in my job, got extra money and a cabin of my own, I worked on a passenger ship and now could spend time praying without being disturbed. Still searching, Kitty and I attended a "Life in the Spirit" seminar and nothing happened to me. So I decided to do the seminar again, a few months went by and one day, as I walked along the road near my home in Kilmore,

Co. Wexford, Ireland, a great weight left me from inside and I started singing in tongues. I had received the Holy Spirit.

Only God knew what was ahead !
Sean continues to share.

"On the twenty second of July, nineteen hundred and ninety seven, my wife Kitty had her hair done in Bridgetown, a photo taken with her brother Joe and a video taken in the garden playing with the grandchildren, an ordinary day and she was enjoying herself. Later on that evening she went to Kilmore Quay, to take part in a concert. She rang home to say that she was not feeling the best, so my daughter Shirley collected her and brought her home. She felt tired and went to bed. I checked on her every few minutes to see if she was ok. She looked asleep but her breathing seemed erratic, while Shirley phoned the doctor Kitty stopped breathing and died. That is how quickly it all happened. She died in peace-no pain, and I thanked God for our life together.

There was more to come !

One day I cycled a distance of one and a half miles to collect my wages. About a half mile from home I felt very tired and stopped at a gap in a field, I could see the cattle in the field, hear the birds singing, feel a slight breeze as the sun shone on my face, a lovely setting. Then all of a sudden, I felt as if someone had slapped me on the back of the head and I doubled up in pain. As I straightened up my hearing went, there was dead silence. A car went by but I did not hear it. My head started to swell up and I said "Jesus help me" I decided that I would try to walk home slowly, you do not meet many cars on a country road. Leaning against a wall in front of a house feeling groggy, I asked the Lord not to let me die on the side of the road like a dog and that my son Shane would be cycling by in about ten minutes. I did not want him to find me in this condition. Eventually a car stopped and a lady asked me if I was ok, I thanked her for stopping and said that I needed an ambulance immediately. I was in Beaumont Hospital within four hours. As they wheeled me to the theatre I thanked God for my life and my family, the doctor told me that I had a ruptured aneurysm, and that he loses one in five patients but not to worry. That is all I remember. I woke up feeling ok, however they had to have a look and see if there were any more aneurysms in my head, they found two more, so back down to theatre. All is well now, I am back on my feet and I thank God every day. John Manning and others had intercessory prayer going on, all the time.

I am a witness to the fact that intercessory prayer is powerful, the living saints praying for those in need. Three months later I had bad depression and a man named Jim McGuire, who John knows well, said "do not let that depression get into you, you are a man of God, an extraordinary man in Jesus Christ. I command that depression to go in Jesus' name". No more depression.

(15)

He had four hours left before they were going to pull the plug of the life support machine, all organs had closed down !

On my travels abroad, I went to visit a friend that I owed some money to. I was repaying about seventy pounds sterling that I had borrowed on my last visit to get parts for my car. She said "come in, you are very welcome, sit down and I will make a cup of tea".

After a while she said "You know that my neighbour's husband is on a life support machine for a while and they intend to switch the machine off in the next five hours. She would be happy, if you went and prayed with her, we were going to phone you for prayer on your help line. The Lord sent you. I went to the neighbour's house, went through the healing and conversion prayer with her, and she asked for the gift of the Holy Spirit. I blessed her with the olive oil and told her that there was a power within her now and that she was to go to the hospital and lay her hands on her husband, for healing saying the same prayer I had said with her. Though in a coma, God's plan would be revealed either way and she would be at peace. She got a phone call early the next morning saying he was ok. Now five years later he is still ok, praise the Lord.

(16)

I am a nurse now retired.

Growing up I was slightly dyslexic, left handed and always sick during my school years. I was a drug addict from medication and an alcoholic !

With my permission, John Manning will tell you my story, if you want to read on.

***

Because it was considered abnormal to be left handed, her mother had instructed her teachers to beat her, so that she would become right handed. She has forgiven her mother and teachers. Things were rough and tough during her early years. After leaving school she went into nursing. As soon as she started to do her midwifery, she started to go downhill rapidly.

They discovered that she had a heart condition called Patent Ductus Arteriosis, which is a hole in the heart, or a hole between two main blood vessels.

There was no heart-surgery in those days,-however she survived and got by. She was called the "puny one" or "yellow hammer" at home because of her yellow skin. Mam and dad were not happy, they were not rich and she was costing them money. In nineteen hundred and seventy five she became very ill and went down to eight stone. They discovered that she had gallstones and appendicitis.

An out of body experience !

She did not go fully out under the anaesthetic, she could feel the knife cutting right through her abdomen and the pain was excruciating. She could not let the anaesthetist know by moving hands or blinking as nothing would move. At one point she got carried away into a most beautiful light, a big light of warmth, where she felt love and joy, then a voice spoke to her and said "Without me there is nothing!" The voice also said, come follow me, or you can stay where you are with your husband and small children. At this point she knew she wanted to be with her husband and children and that God had spoken. He showed her the doctors and nurses in the theatre standing still as little black specks. The surgeons hand actually stopped and seemed to be controlled by God. Her memory has faded over the years, however she can never forget the experience. It is, I suppose similar to my, own rainbow experience, I will never forget that. She never told anyone until she and I prayed together for healing down along the road of life.

When she got married the doctors told her that she would have to marry a very considerate man, and not have too many children.

Her troubles were only starting?

She ended up marrying an epileptic-he had never told her that he was on medication. He deceived her and she has only learned to forgive in recent times. In the part of Ireland where she was brought up, epileptics were looked down on, and they were brought up to be afraid of them, and not talk to them or go near them in case they would fall on you. The attacks took place at home and she was always there to help him. The great worry was that he would get an attack while driving the car, which he needed for his work. She was always angry with him for lying. She also knew that he suffered as much as she did. He was totally in denial about his situation. She could not trust him

She wanted to get out of the world !

She was always a strong person, even though she had health problems. She was strong with the family, getting the children to school, making sure that they had a good education and always doing what she considered was right. In nineteen ninety, she just felt that she not want to be here anymore. She was feeling suicidal, very depressed, partly menopausal and started drinking to help her sleep, and over a short period became a complete alcoholic. First thing every morning she had the DT's, she went through the whole works, she depended totally on alcohol to get through the day and night. She was a complete mess and would stand on the landing of their fine big house and throw empty bottles at her husband and children, they usually went out the garage door, the front door exit was too dangerous. It was hellish for her, she wanted to get out of it, she a qualified medical sister, who could she turn to. She continued to drink even more until one day she was on all fours, was out of her mind to a great degree and did eventually go to her doctor and confessed that she had a drink problem. The doctor was brilliant. She cried and cried, he took her under his wing and said that he would help her get all right. He wanted to send her to hospital, but she said "no so", he detoxed her. Her children were aware of her problem, but her husband did not want to know. Her own family brothers sisters etc. despised her. She found the AA meetings just great but knows now that there was something missing which was the Holy Spirit.

Even off the drink she was depressed,
and unable to face work !

"As I came out of mass one morning in a country town, having held a healing meeting the night before, I was introduced to my friend as she is now and whose story you have just read, by a lady who just said "John this lady needs help". I introduced myself as an evangelist told her what I do. We linked arms, and we walked slowly to her house praying in a whisper as we went with all the people passing by wondering what was going on. I stayed with my new friend in Christ for a few hours, drinking tea and reading the scriptures. I took my new found friend through the healing and conversion prayer and before I left for Dublin, she received a great healing and conversion, she was on her way now. I phoned every second day and she phoned every fourth day to share the scriptures. This went on for eighteen months, no one knew about it only herself, me and the Lord. Real healing is in the Word of God. It becomes a living Word when spoken by a Spirit filled person.

Jesus is with her now every day, and can be with you, the reader, if you have a problem. My friend has been able to forgive her husband after all these years, her children adore her and she and her husband have gone places as a couple. They had lived in hell for years, and spent the last four great years together up to the time of her husband's death. She is a super lady and can walk tall. She is what I call an intercessor, she can pray for people that are as sick as she was. God hears her prayers. She has the gift of healing that comes from the Lord. I declare Jesus before men and women with problems, and Jesus proclaims me before his father in heaven. God allowed my friend to go through what she went through all those years. She knows now like I do, that we are made for the next world, and can only overcome the things of the flesh in this world by the power of the Holy Spirit.

(17)

Her dad, her mam and brother were alcoholics, and very mean to this lovely lady.

Her mam died, her dad died, her brother died, her husband died, and one of her two daughters died. She went into deep depression, and had not pulled back the curtains on any of the windows in her house for years. Her only living daughter had heart problems. With things so bad she said it was like being hit by an army tank. The story often reminded me of that great movie called "Great Expectations". A four story house in darkness-morning noon and night. Her brother who died tragically was an alcoholic like their mam and dad. I often prayed with him, he loved the scriptures. He told his sister that she should talk with me about her depression, she would say to him, sure he is probably worse than you, another waster. "I phoned on numerous occasions to talk with her, at least ten times, eventually I really prayed and asked the Lord if this was the time for him to open the door to Jesus for her. I said I will not phone anymore, until I know in my spirit that she will say yes to a prayer over the phone. Eventually I did phone, she agreed to say the healing and conversion prayer with me, during the prayer time I said to her, that God wanted to pour out His Holy Spirit on all women and children, and would she like to receive the Holy

Spirit. She said she would. Having addressed a lot of issues like hate, resentment, anger towards man and God, of which she repented. I then asked her to go into each room, and draw back the curtains in Jesus' name saying "Heavenly Father now that I have invited Jesus the light of the world into my life, by the power of the Holy Spirit I will allow day light into my house". She did and has never looked back since, praise God. Her only living daughter had a great miracle happen to her. Nothing is impossible for God, just ask in Jesus' name. So why don't we see more signs and wonders, when Jesus says "Signs and wonders will follow those who believe"? If you do not see miracles in your life, stop a while and ask why not. Dolores and I got to know her soon after the miracle, and are friends ever since. Little Amanda loves her like we all do.

" Make haste slowly"

Six years ago I Paul changed almost overnight from a very happy go lucky chap into a suicidal depressive. I firmly believe the catalyst for this dramatic change was down to a severe reaction to an anaesthetic, received during a minor operation. However in the context of this story, the cause is unimportant, only the solution.

My illness resulted in me being hospitalised in St. Patrick's Hospital, where I was given what seemed like a conveyor belt of drugs and electric shock treatment all to no avail.

Released back into the big bad world, my depression got worse, leaving me fearful of losing my wife, my two lovely boys, my home, my job, my pride and my life. There was no let up at all in my emotional state as I became more frightened and bewildered.

As conventional treatment had failed I began to seek out more outlandish alternatives like you see advertised, where they claim cures for everything from the common cold to cancer. After trying a few of these so called cures, my depression was not to lighten but my bank balance did.

I first encountered John Manning, at a conference on healing. He had noticed my dejection with what was going on at this conference and invited me to his home. He pointed out that he personally had no power, but that there was a power available to all just for the asking.

My first impression was that this guy was wacko, gay or both. In fact the fact, that he did not take money made me more nervous and suspicious, however, His humility and pleasant demeanour won me over.

We were two ordinary

joes asking Jesus for a dig out ?

"Our first meeting was a very innocuous, low key affair as were all our sessions over the next while, ending in very gentle prayer, no fanfare, no flashing lights just two ordinary people asking Jesus for a dig out. The results were also less dramatic, a half of a percent at a time and as they say an inch is as good as a mile, if it is in the right direction. Nothing else I had tried could lay claim to any improvement.

I should be honest and say that I always had a belief in Jesus, John somehow made him more accessible, my faith enhanced, as did my mood. The, rest like they say is history. After a year I began to feel myself normal again, more enlightened and understanding.

John Manning is a close friend now, whether he likes it or not. I thank God for that chance encounter or was it. ? Since I wrote to John, I have been able to cope with my dad's death and come from darkness to light. I am free and I thank God in Jesus' name.

(19)

The Ouija Board
brought misery and suicide into this Joan's life and may to others who get involved.

"For the purpose of this true story call me Joan. I cry out every day thanking God for the gift of the Holy Spirit, and for the hope and peace I experience in my life now. Always rejecting ways behind me which upset my life and caused me and others deep anguish and pain. One of these practices, before I invited

Jesus to come and live in me after repentance, was the practice of the Ouija Board.

It brought utter chaos and misery into my life, my home and suicide to one party. It is counterfeit fun. When all traces of any contact with this practice was prayed out and repented of, like John has explained, how to do it in this book, hands were laid on me and I could feel something leave me. God the Father had set me free in Jesus' name. And I was baptised in the Holy Spirit. I strongly advise that anyone who is involved to get out. If your are invited to a party that has anything to do with spiritualism, the occult, the Ouija Board, fortune telling, tarot card reading etc., stay away. Jesus turned water into wine for me, and will do the same for you if you let Him".

AMANDA SAYS **love** IS

This little girl of so many special needs, is full of the Holy Spirit content and happy as reflected in her eyes, smile and body language. She shares in love and understands the following things that granda has shared with her about God, which may bring hope and comfort to others with special needs.

Love is when mammy, nanna or granda walk by my room and always say hello.

Love is when my mammy puts me on my feed machine before she goes to work at 5 a.m.

Love is when nanna and granda take over after mammy goes to work and gets me ready for school before 8.30.

Love is when Michael, the CRC bus driver calls at my house with Theresa his helper along with Will, Alan, Meggin, Lee, Adam and Jemma my school pals to go to school in all the traffic.

Love is the way I am treated in school by helpers, teachers, nurses, doctors and staff, who look after my needs while they may have needs and problems of their own.

Love is when I cannot turn in my bed if I get a cramp, then mammy, nanna or granda turn me and make me comfortable.

Love is when the other children on the bus ask granda to say a prayer with them, when they do not feel well, and I join him.

Love is when granda, who reads the bible to me, shows me a picture of Jesus holding a little child in His arms and asks me who the child is and I say "e" "e" meaning me.

Love is when mammy can see the love granda and nanna have for her, when she sees the love they have for me.

Love is when I put my tongue out and they know that I need a cold spoon or a little drop of water on my tongue, or a drink from my special drinking mug and they give it to me.

Love is when I go for a walk in my wheel chair with mammy, granda, and Alicia our neighbour, and people say "hello".

Love is when mammy, nanna or granda give my hands and face a wash with a hot towel in the mornings before they dress me.

Love is when granda who is big and strong and I am getting bigger, lifts me up in his arms and gives me a big hug and tells me he loves me, as nanna does as I lie in the bed, not feeling afraid.

Love is the way the nurses, doctors and staff in the Rotunda Hospital Dublin looked after me after I was born. Now that I am older the nurses, doctors' and staff in Temple Street Hospital, Dublin do the same thing, especially when my feeding tube falls out of my tummy and they put a new one in without hurting me.

Love is when I tell mammy that I am sad because I cannot do the things other children can do. Mammy told granda who then took me in his arms and prayed with me telling me that lots of men women and children in the world are sad and always will be because of evil people, even though **they** can do the things I cannot do. They do not know Jesus or the Holy Spirit who lives in me like I do, so they do not have that peace that defies all human understanding. We said a prayer and thanked God in Jesus' name. I was at peace knowing that God loved me and allowed my condition, but did not cause it and had a plan for me and would fulfill it in His time.

Love is that mammy, nanna and granda know that I belong to God first, then to them. When my aunty Maura who makes me laugh, or uncles, cousins, neighbours and friends like Marie, Paddy, Alicia, Aidan or Gerry drop by like Mary Murphy did (who is gone to heaven now) to say "hello" to me where I live now with mammy, nanna and granda.

Love is when Dr. Burbridge looks after me with little or no notice and when he is away, Dr. Howlett or Dr. Kelly take over with the help of Angela, Elizabeth and Mary.

Love is when granda, who introduced me to Charlie Landsborough's song called "My forever friend", sings and dances with me in his arms till his back gives in.

Love is when I pray with granda for all the people that have prayed for me over the last eight years and to God for allowing me to survive when it was thought I would not last eight minutes.

Love is when granda tells me that God knew me before he put me together in mammy's tummy and I can believe it.

Love is when granda cannot play as much golf as he would like, because he helps look after me.

Love is when my best friend Amy comes to visit with her mam, dad and baby Sean.

There is no need to walk alone.

Walk with God.

CAN YOU COPE WITH YOUR PROBLEM ?

Is it listed or mentioned in the testimonies ?

Before you consider the pain **YOU** are suffering and the loneliness you feel right now, read the following stories of people of the past - just to mention a few. Read about their sufferings and compare their stories with the testimonies of the people in this book, who have also survived and overcome.

JOB, a good man, who suffered total disaster- lost all his children and property and was inflicted with a repulsive disease. (Job 1/13 -19)

MARY, the mother of Jesus on her own, her husband Joseph who was dead, was not there to comfort her at the cross, as Jesus died in front of her eyes, and a spear or a sword pierced her soul. We are all living souls, she survived! So will you and I, when we trust in God as she did.

KING DAVID, his young son died on the seventh day. David knew he could not bring him back to life. He said "I will go to him, but he will not return to me". Did he mean that he would go and visit at his son's grave, or see him in heaven? (2 Samuel 12/23).

LAZARUS, did not ask to be brought back to life. He eventually died like we all will. Miracles are only temporary. (John 11/38-44)

PAUL, the Apostle, who never met Jesus in the flesh, was disfigured, felt unloved and suffered a lot of hardship. (Gal. 4/15)

ABRAHAM, in obedience to God, was going to kill his son Isaac when God intervened. (Gen. 22/12)

THE MAMMIES AND DADDIES' of the two-year old boy babies that King Herod had killed around the time Jesus was born. GOD, the creator of Heaven and Earth, knew what he was doing by allowing the children to die; their Spirit body returned to God, who allowed but did not cause their deaths. (Matt. 2/16)

When I see or hear of children being aborted, mammies having miscarriages or still-births', of children being slaughtered or starved to death because of famine, I get sad. I believe all children belong to God, we only have a loan of them. The children's spirit bodies and souls return to God no matter how they die. He takes Spirit beings home to a better place, this is how He populates heaven. My faith in God and my understanding of the scriptures, softens the blow and helps me cope with the sadness. **JOHN THE BAPTIST,** who bore witness to the light and was beheaded in prison, imagine how he felt. (Matt. 14/10) **GOD THE FATHER,** who suffered as he watched Jesus, his only son take on the sins of the world, before his awful death on the cross and JESUS who thought his Father had forsaken him. How often did I think God had forsaken me! **SO I ASK,** who are we to moan! We are not the only generation to suffer since the fall from grace of our first parents and we will not be the last.

Having reflected on what people of the past who were close to God suffered.

now

CONSIDER **YOUR** LONELINESS AND THE LONELINESS OF PRESENT CENTURY MEN WOMEN AND CHILDREN.

***

MOST OF THE FOLLOWING

CONDITIONS THAT CAUSE

LONELINESS,

COME FROM THE QUESTIONS PEOPLE

HAVE ASKED OF ME OVER THE YEARS.

YOU MIGHT ASK THE SAME

QUESTIONS IN RELATION TO LIFE,

DEATH, DISABILITIES,

SICKNESS AND RELIGION

No matter who you are, what you have, or who you know, if your physical body is unhealthy or deformed in anyway, minus limbs, un-sighted, unable to walk or talk before you die, your immortal spirit body, that Jesus knew before he put you together in your mother's tummy, is perfect. The mortal body is temporary perfect or not, will turn to dust. We have problems because we are born of the seed /flesh of man. If you are in a wheel-chair now you will not need it in heaven or hell. The spirit body is perfect in either place.

THE TRUE TESTIMONIES IN THIS BOOK WILL COVER, LIKE A BLANKET, MOST OF THE CONDITIONS THAT CAUSE LONELINESS.

Consider-The loneliness of the bereaved - the loneliness of the gambler - the loneliness of the separated - the loneliness of the alcoholic-the loneliness of the divorced - the loneliness of the rejected - the loneliness of the children, when mammy or daddy has gone off with someone else - the loneliness of the unmarried mother, particularly if she has a sick or handicapped child and feels that God is getting his own back on her for having a baby outside of marriage, out of the sin of fornication, a forgivable sin.

the loneliness of the sick and dying, when all around them are well - the loneliness of mammy, dad, brothers and sisters when a child goes missing, (like Mary when Jesus went walk about) - the loneliness of a person with aids - the loneliness of a person in prison - the loneliness of a person, male or female, confused about their sexual feelings or sexuality - the loneliness of people who suffer from various kinds of depression or mental illness - the loneliness of people who do not feel they belong - the loneliness of the family of a suicide victim - the loneliness of families who have experienced cot deaths.

No reconciliation before death.

The loneliness of a person when someone has died and there was no reconciliation, between family or friend - the loneliness of the mammy after or before an abortion - the loneliness of nuns, priests and brothers and others trying to cope with chastity - the loneliness of the unmarried who were never asked - the loneliness of those with low self esteem - the loneliness of those who have no education and cannot read or write - the loneliness of those who are blind - the loneliness of the deaf - the loneliness of those who cannot walk or talk - the loneliness of those adopted or fostered - the loneliness of the broken hearted - the loneliness of those contemplating suicide - the loneliness of the physically deformed - the loneliness of the man whose wife will not have intercourse with him anymore after she had her last baby, and he struggles with the idea of going to a prostitute, or having a girl friend - the loneliness of a mammy that has to carry a dead child the full term - the loneliness of the mam and dad who do not talk and live together.

The loneliness of the rich man or woman.

The loneliness of the rich man or woman who has everything but no inner peace and is afraid to die - the loneliness of the academic where the pride of the intellect which is a gift prevents him from believing in God - the loneliness of the married couple when love has gone dead - the loneliness of the mammy or daddy whose children suffer from hereditary health problems particularly depression and mental illness that was never mentioned or disclosed before marriage and did not manifest itself till the children became teenagers.

The loneliness and guilt of people with sexually transmitted diseases.

The loneliness of priests, brothers and nuns, who when they were ordained, were told they could never marry (celibacy) and could not be relieved of the vow of chastity, no man or woman is relieved of that vow, every man and woman, nun, priest or not has to keep the vow of chastity, or they commit the sin of fornication, unlawful sexual intercourse. - the loneliness of the priests that were told once a priest always a priest (life long priesthood eternal) I believe this applied to Jesus not to man.

The loneliness of priests, pastors, clergymen, nuns, brothers etc.

The loneliness of people outside the Roman Catholic Church who were told they could not go to heaven if they died, then Vatican II said that you could be saved outside of the Roman Catholic Church - the loneliness and anger of some priests when this statement was made, who would love to have been married, have a family and have served God also - the loneliness of autistic children - the loneliness of rape victims - the loneliness of the epileptic - the loneliness of the person with dyslexia - the loneliness of MS and ME sufferers and carers - the loneliness of those who suffer from obesity - the loneliness of the mentally ill -

The loneliness of the down syndrome child or any special needs child, mam, dad brothers and sisters, who worry for the future of the child.

The loneliness the person with anorexia - the loneliness of those who have no faith or hope - the loneliness of those in denial - the loneliness of those who feel unfulfilled - the loneliness of the mam and dad after a still birth, or miscarriage -the loneliness of those in prison behind bars - the loneliness of the person with social phobia - the loneliness of the mammy or daddy and children caught up in domestic violence the hidden sin in Ireland that can scar mammies, daddies and children emotionally for ever - the loneliness of the children of the past who are adults now, who suffered sexual abuse at the hands of families, employees of state schools, churches, institutions and orphanages of all denominations. THIS CRIME WILL CONTINUE TO GO ON because of man's sinful and fallen nature until Jesus comes back. We must be watchful at all times.

***

IF YOUR PRAYERS ARE NOT ANSWERED, OR YOUR LONELINESS CONTINUES, REMEMBER

THAT NO - CAN BE AN ANSWER

JUSTICE OR HEALING DELAYED IS NOT JUSTICE OR HEALING DENIED

In 2 Cor. **The Apostle Paul talks about the thorn in his flesh. Are we all like Paul ?**

Paul says that he prayed three times to the Lord about this <u>physical</u> ailment, and asked him to take it away. But his answer was:- "My grace is sufficient for you, for my power is made perfect in weakness". Paul went on to say "Therefore I will boast all the more gladly of my weaknesses, so that Christ's power may rest in me". *When the same power rests in us, then we can cope.* * No one really knows what the thorn in Paul's flesh was. **Read Gal. 4/13-14-15-16.** and see what you think "As you know, it was because of an illness that I first preached the Gospel to you. Even though my illness was a trial to you, you did not treat me with contempt or scorn. Instead, you welcomed me as if I was angel of God, as if I were Christ himself. What has happened to all your joy? I can testify that, if you could have done so, you would have torn out your own eyes and given them to me". *I believe he had an eye problem, that made him feel ugly ?* Paul coped, does it matter what his problem was. We can be distracted trying to understand things that we do not need to know. If you can establish the cause of your loneliness in any of the conditions I have mentioned, then pray it out in Jesus' name like the people of the testimonies in this book did, and ask for God's will to be done in your life. Some Gay people and others that I know, have identified their condition with Paul's thorn in the flesh. Lonely or not, we live in darkness, until we repent for our sins and invite Jesus come live in us. Ask for the gift of the Holy Spirit to fill that cavity of loneliness in you, then ask for the gift of faith in Jesus' name. I, and millions more have come from darkness into the light, so can you, just like the Apostle Paul did who like you and I never met Jesus in the flesh. I believe every human being is lonely until they come into a personal relationship with Jesus.

It all seemed to stand still at one stage for my

wife Dolores, this may happen to you also.

Half way into Dolores' healing, it just seemed to stop. Dolores and I prayed about it and said to the Lord the following "Lord if this is your plan for Dolores, that she not progress any further, that is ok with us. However, if you want to continue her healing for your own reasons that is ok also". We were praying within the will of the father. Just like that, the progress continued and the reason for the miracle is told in little Amanda's true story as recorded in this book on page 125.

I HAVE PRAYED THE LIVING WORD INTO THOUSANDS OF SITUATIONS, SIMILAR TO THOSE I HAVE JUST QUOTED IN THE TESTIMONIES AND ON PAGES 183-187 AND LOTS MORE. IF YOU HAVE A PROBLEM NOT LISTED, JUST ADD IT ON. I KNOW FROM MY OWN EXPERIENCE THAT JESUS IS THE ONLY ONE THAT CAN FILL THAT CAVITY OF LONELINESS **AND** FEAR WITHIN YOU, AND *HEAL* THE *CAUSE,* AS THE TRUE TESTIMONIES IN THIS BOOK CLAIM.

The worst sickness of all to have ?

I have been asked on a few occasions what sickness, do I believe is the worst to have. I believe anything that has to do with the mind. You can be diagnosed with various forms of depression early in life, be miserable and live till you are eighty. However your spirit body that returns to God (or to hell) when you physically die, lives for ever in heaven without depression or in hell with depression, particularly after you find out that you were deceived and someone put you on the bus of religion, that said it was going to purgatory, which I do not believe exists. We are immortal we never really die and as we are Spirit beings we must exist somewhere.

(2 Cor. 7/10 -NIV)

It is written in the word of God "That Godly sorrow brings repentance that leads to salvation and leaves no regret, but worldly sorrow brings death".

Contentment can only be found outside of material things in Jesus!

YOU AND YOU

CAN OVERCOME, LIKE THE PEOPLE OF THE TESTIMONIES IN THIS BOOK DID.

(Rev. 12/11)

"They overcame him by the blood of the Lamb and by the word of their testimony; they did not love their lives so much as to shrink from death".

I explain the above scripture this way... The Lamb is Jesus who by His death on the cross set us free of fear and sin etc. The people of the testimonies in this book were not afraid, they did not want to hang onto their old way of life (do you ?) they died to their old ways, and the sinful desires of the flesh had no power over them anymore.

God's Word does not have to be updated, like most things to day because of technology advancements. The Word never changes from generation to generation. A thousand years from now or at anytime you can speak the same Word that is timeless, to the problems and concerns of people in any generation, until Jesus comes back.

From my experience, the loneliness that people suffer is closely linked with self-pity, the center of depression which can be caused by a blocked goal, like promotion or being unsuccessful in life, married but with no children or any of the many things mentioned in this book. I believe if you heal the emotions, you will cope, and improve the quality of your life, the lives of others around you and prevent and heal a lot of sickness. If you are okay while on medication, and not if you don't take it, then you need to be "born again". Ask for the gift of the Holy Spirit, the gift of faith, wisdom and discernment **to stay** on your medication and cope, if the miracle you ask for does not happen.

Say the following prayer, whether you go to church or not, before you read any further.

"Heavenly Father I repent for all my sins in Jesus' name. Do not let me retain any sin of unforgiveness towards any person, send your Holy Spirit to comfort those I have hurt and set me free of all activities not of you, including gambling, occult practices, new age activities, fortune telling, tarot card reading, enneagram etc. "I confirm, and now believe as an adult, all the prayers said over me at infant baptism. I accept your

only Son Jesus as my Lord and Saviour. I mean what I say from my heart. (having said this, then you are "born again", an adult conversion). I now ask you for the gift of the Holy Spirit and accept it, the gift of faith, wisdom and discernment to help me understand and come into the knowledge of your Word, so that I can cope and overcome. Heal my spiritual blindness and deafness. "I know Lord what you have done for John and his wife Dolores and others, you will do for me".

*

Suffering humanity must turn to someone, or some thing in their search for inner healing and peace. Let that person be Jesus, not dead saints, ritualistic contaminated doctrine, or pious opinions that have no power and leave people disillusioned, and blame God for their condition. In the past we passed on the doctrine of the Roman catholic church, our Protestant brethren passed on the doctrine of their denomination. On and on it went from generation to generation, denomination to denomination. You can hand on doctrine, but you cannot hand on faith, it is a gift to be received, ask for it. *You have nothing to lose.*

CHAPTER 2

The Holy Spirit enables me to encourage you, to ask and receive, if you find it hard to cope.

STRAIGHT TALK

I believe that the message is more important than the messenger. I write exactly as I speak so the results should be the same.

I am a sinner, an evangelist and a recipient of this forgotten power, no fancy words just plain God talk from an ordinary guy. I am not a scholar or a writer, priest, pastor, brother or preacher, only in the biblical sense. I am publishing and typing this book myself. I had to learn how to use the computer from scratch with lots of help from friends. I am responsible to God for what I say. You may not like what I say or the way I say things, my grammar, spelling or punctuation, quotes may be missing, there may be a full point before the ? If there are please forgive me. I am an ordinary layman come fisherman, asking many questions. I am writing and sharing in love an experience that changed my life, and the life of others that could not cope until I shared my experience with them, the same may help you. The Apostle Paul in 1 Cor. 2/4, said that his message and his preaching were not with wise and persuasive words, but with a demonstration of the Spirit's power, so that your faith might not rest in man's wisdom, but on God's power. This book is not about John Manning but about Jesus. My testimony brought great comfort to those I shared with including my own family. Paul's confidence as a preacher did not rest on intellectual and oratorical ability, but on the power of the Holy Spirit. Some things I say may be repetitive as in Scripture, and essential to make a point, particularly in the area of questions and answers comparing pious opinions and heresy with truth. You may not want to read all of this book. However, someone may have asked a question you would like to ask, the answer could be interesting. Slip to the question and answer section at the back of the book and have a look if you want. ***I know what I do and how I do it works.*** A spade is a spade and what Jesus says is the truth. False prophets not in the Spirit had led me to mistake their pious opinions and fancy words, which were ineffective for the Word of God.

(Mark 13/31)

"Heaven and Earth will pass away, but My Words will never pass away".

I have used the bibles and books listed at the front of this book together with personal revelation as my sources of information. I now know that God lives outside of time and that His Word is timeless.

My further testimony.

I never thought I was a sinner, as I did not rob handbags, cars or houses and went to confession once a week. I exchanged sins regularly with my pals, so that the priest would not be bored hearing the same sins every week. I also attended to all my religious duties and rituals, and I know now, wrongly believing that I was okay with God, that if I was to die at any time I would go straight to heaven because of my attention to religious duty and dead works, meaning "Acts that led to death" (Hebs. 6/1) of which I repented .

I believe that the "isms" of the man- made churches have contaminated the Word of God and institutionalised a lot of their member's by the doctrine they taught.

I thank God for my spiritual awakening, the good things and the bad things in my life, and for the time frame or window of opportunity that He gave me, to examine the religion and doctrine that I was brought up with. This book is about my findings and experiences. I have met people in other denominations that have done the same thing, they "are born again" and we are brothers and sisters in Christ, living stones, the real church.

My doctrine prevented me from being in touch with other Christians. I was blind to truth and ignorant of the world and its questions of which some are mentioned in this book. I, like many more in my denomination and other denominations, have become catholic as described in the creed. I was a carnal, sinful, unspiritual, worldly Christian, a creature of the flesh. (1Cor. 3/4 For when one says "I follow Paul," and another, "I follow Apollos," are you not mere men?) I was captive to sin by my Adam and Eve inherited sinful nature which I believe is original sin. The desires of the flesh I was born with, keep me in conflict with my new Christ-like nature. However Christ freed me and can free you too, to live in the power of the Holy Spirit; then you can cope. It is your choice. We either walk in the flesh or in the Spirit.

Faith is a gift to be asked for and received

MOSES 3300 years ago had his back to the Red Sea when he told the Hebrews to trust in God. They did, God intervened and they were saved.

I DID THE SAME THING 3286 YEARS LATER, using the Word of the same God, when my back was to the wall, and I was finding it hard to cope with my wife's confining and painful illness and my business problems.

The true testimonies in this book, pages 1 to 178 can be verified, and will cover like a blanket, most of the problems you will experience in life. The same God of Abraham and Moses intervened for me and will for you also, if you pray and worship in Spirit and truth and be "born again". Do not feel so bad, Nicodemus the scholar had a problem understanding "the born" again expression, that is explained in this book. I have met and prayed with theologians who told me that they had no faith, they did not have to tell me. I knew the minute I started to pray with them. As we prayed we thanked God for the gift of the intellect God had given them and prayed out the pride of the intellect and repented of it by rebuking it in Jesus' name. Pride, the catalyst that started the fire in hell, in any shape or form is a sin. I do not have the mind of a child in business, however, I do have the mind of a child as a creature, compared to the mind of the creator.

I now know that there is a divine order for miracles, signs and wonders to happen.

Dolores and I, along with the people of the true testimonies recorded in this book, have experienced this order and moved from darkness into the light. We speak from a depth of knowledge and experience, and share in love with anyone who wants to read this book, why the God of our religion did not answer our prayers and may not be answering yours.

Darkness is the absence of light Jesus is the light.

To be depressed, lonely or worried for whatever the reason and not be able to cope, is to be in darkness, which is the absence of light. I know, I have been there.

I discovered how to pray and get results.

I always pray within the will of the Father and repent, saying sorry to Him in Jesus' name for my sins. I have learned that God sent His Word to heal us. He will watch over His Word that we send back to Him when we pray. His Word will be sustained by the Holy Spirit because it is truth. The Holy Spirit will not sustain pious opinions no matter how flowery they sound.

On page 588 of the Catechism of the Roman catholic church (2769) and I quote "In Baptism and confirmation, the handing on (traditio) of the Lord's Prayer signifies new birth into divine life. Since Christian prayer is our speaking to God with, every **Word** of God, those who are 'born anew' through the living and divine Word of

God learn to invoke their Father by **one** Word HE always hears *(His Word)*. They can hence forth do so, for the seal of the Holy Spirit's anointing is indelibly placed on their hearts, ears, lips, indeed their whole filial (meaning that befitting a son or daughter) being".

Dolores and I survived so can you.

We discovered that our knowledge of the Word of God, prior our to conversion was incomplete, is yours ?

Dolores and I suffered and felt the loneliness of people who could not **cope,** as you will gather from our testimonies.

For us faith in God is **not** a theory anymore, it is a proven experience, so we can talk about it and know that our knowledge of the Word of God prior to our conversion was incomplete.

We have shared with people from most parts of the world, at meetings, on our telephone help line and on radio. If someone from any of the two thousand five hundred and thirty four families, who phoned for prayer, or a chat, over the last number of years is not touched by the

Lord during the prayer time, I will not hear from that family anymore. **God builds our ministry.** However when the Lord does touch them, you hear from their friends, relations and neighbours far and wide, they tell one another. Some have gone back to church because they wanted to, are not bored anymore and can separate truth from pious opinions. The Word goes out like a perfume, that is if you speak *God's Word* into a situation, **not your own.**

I sow or water seeds in Jesus' name and God makes them grow on this tract of land called the earth, in His time, not yours or mine. (2 Cor.9-10) God gives me the seed to sow. "Now he who supplies seed to the sower and bread for food will also supply and increase your store of seed and will enlarge the harvest of your righteousness". Which I believe means the Holy Spirit flowing freely in your life to produce signs and wonders, that holy rituals cannot produce.

(John 5-39) "You study the Scriptures, because you think that in them you will find eternal life. And these very Scriptures speak about ME! you are not willing TO COME TO ME! in order to have eternal life". So I ask, - if we cannot find Jesus or eternal life by reading the Scriptures, what chance have we by saying rosaries, doing novenas, wearing scapulars, praying to Mary, Padre Pio, St. Therese or following her bones, climbing mountains or visiting holy places? God was Mary's first love. God must be our first love also, it is He who brings us close to Jesus. Know one and you know the other.

I believe all of these holy pious things are baggage from the past, bringing us into a comfort zone, until we need the next fix. On and on it goes, no power, no healing, no hope, no Jesus in your life, so we stay in darkness. If the focus is on your problem, or on any name, other than the name of Jesus, then the Spirit will not move.

The blind man cried out saying (Luke 18/38), "Jesus Son of David, have mercy on me!" he did not ask to be healed first, he asked for mercy then he was healed. When I challenge people who pray to Mary, Padre Pio or Matt Talbot, asking them to intercede for them with God, they say they are not, they are asking them to ask Jesus to ask God for what they want. I believe they are in error.

Jesus says that you cannot come to Him unless the Father draws you. (1 Tim. 2/5) "For there is one God and one mediator between God and men, the man Christ Jesus, who gave himself as ransom for all men".

God spoke creation into existence.

"In the beginning was the Word"

The Word made flesh, in which Jesus is present, is flawless and should not be peddled. This is why, as an evangelist, I stick strictly to the Word of God, for when I do I see signs and wonders, So will you.

God's Word and His promises are timeless and will never change. Jesus brought the Kingdom of God to His followers, His living saints and fulfilled the prophesy mentioned in Daniel 7/18 around 530 BC.

My Scriptural understanding of physical death, no matter what the cause, helped me answer the following.

IF I AM PHYSICALLY BLIND,

HAVE NO HANDS OR LEGS,

WHAT WILL I BE LIKE IN HEAVEN

WHEN I DIE ?

A revealed understanding of Scripture helped me cope with my mam and dads' physical death as I shared in my testimony. I share the following with you in love. The Spirit body of all human beings is perfect and indwells the flesh body for a period of time determined by God and leaves instantly at death for judgement or reward. The physical flesh body may not be perfect, it may be un-sighted have no hands, legs or whatever. I believe that there is no lapse of time between death of the flesh and the Spirit body being with God. This I believe also applies to all adults, children of still births, miscarriages, abortions and those murdered or who die from natural causes, accidents or ethnic cleansing.

A STILL BIRTH

My Mother had a still birth many years ago. The outer shell of flesh, that covered the spirit body of the person in her tummy perished. However I believe that the spirit body and soul of the person returned to God to be fulfilled. Fully grown in every way, like God had ordained and to know mam and dad in the present heaven or paradise, sixty seven years later and be able to see Jesus as He is with the eyes of his/her spirit body. God populates heaven with spirit beings made in His Spirit image and likeness, He is not flesh.

(Psalm 139/13-16 Lev. 20/2)

ABORTION

We sacrifice our babies to the God of convenience.

(LUKE 23/28)

We are weeping for ourselves and our children as Jesus had predicted.

Abortion is a very serious but forgiveable sin. God allows the mammy to abort the plan God had for the child in this world, and He fulfils the plan *He had ordained for the child in the next, as the child's, spirit-body (a living soul) returns to God.*

I believe that children before and after in the womb have identity. God knew them before and after he put them together in the mammy's tummy, there is a progression of development from the beginning. Abortion is a blot on our society and makes a statement that as humans we are worth nothing. I believe it is because we lack the knowledge of the Word of God.

Leviticus 20/2 tells me of the ancient worship of Molech which often involved child sacrifice, bestiality, active homosexuality and incest, to please Molech in the life and worship of ancient Israel about 1445 BC. Abortion and religious practices in all generations that are not Scripture based, break the bond of holiness between God and man. In modern times we sacrifice our babies to the God of convenience.

MAMMY- SEE QUESTION AND ANSWER SECTION FOR A SPECIAL PRAYER ON PAGES 377-8 FOR MAMMIES WHO HAVE HAD AN ABORTION.

Mammies, if you have had a miscarriage, still birth or an abortion, thank God for allowing you to populate heaven with a Spirit being made in His Spirit image and likeness.

*

A MISCARRIAGE

God cancels the plan he had for the child in this world, because He knows best, and fulfils the plan for the child in the next as the spirit body and soul returns to God in all fullness as he has ordained.

DEATH BY NATURAL CAUSES, OR DEATH CAUSED BY MURDER, WAR OR ETHNIC CLEANSING, IT DOES NOT MATTER. GOD'S ROAD MAP FOR THE SPIRIT BODY THAT IS A LIVING SOUL AS IT JOURNEYS THROUGH THE HEAVENS IS WELL SIGN POSTED IN THE BIBLE FOR ALL WHO WISH TO FOLLOW.

IF YOU DON'T WISH TO FOLLOW, GOD STILL LOVES YOU, WHETHER YOU LOVE HIM OR NOT AND HE WOULD LIKE YOU TO GET TO KNOW HIM.

IF YOUR CHILD WAS MURDERED

The murderer destroys the flesh that covers the spirit body of the child on this planet and shortens the life span, but could never harm the spirit body that returns to God to be fulfilled as God had planned for the next.

All children belong to God until they become aware, or are convicted of their first sin. I believe that quite a lot of people can remember their first sin, and the guilt that went with it. When Adam and Eve realized they were naked in the garden, they too were convicted. We only have a loan of one another in physical form in this world.

SUICIDE

The person who commits suicide, harms the physical body, but cannot harm the spirit body or soul, we are living souls. Neither do we know what the person has said to God before the act. I believe God gives everyone a window of opportunity to repent, no matter what the circumstances. We are not to judge who goes to heaven and who does not when they die. Only God knows who is in heaven. There is time from the bridge to the water below, from the river bank to the water, from the platform to the track or what ever. To repent it takes less than a second (it is a thought) to say sorry, you say it in your heart, your inner being, and has nothing to do with your mouth or the pump in your chest.

*See special prayer for families of suicide victims in question and answer section on pages 339-340-341.

How often have I heard and read the

following words, and never understood...do

you ?

"For your faithful people, Lord, life is changed, not ended. And when the flesh body the earthly dwelling place of our immortal spirit body lies in death, we gain an everlasting_dwelling place in heaven".

(Genesis 3/6)

The earthly temporary dwelling place for our spirit body that never dies (immortal) is our flesh body, that dies within 120 years and returns to dust. When we die our spirit body (as in God's spirit image and likeness) returns to God to live in a spirit world, for which we were created and will include all children that do not have to be "born again" until after they commit their first sin. Flesh cannot enter heaven or hell. Our temporary flesh body makes us visible to one another in this world.

My son is twenty two years old and Down Syndrome, will he be a Down Syndrome in heaven ?

The physical appearance of a Down Syndrome person is different from others in the flesh. But the spirit body is perfect as God wants it to be. If only other people in our society could be as loving and caring as a Down Syndrome person, the world would be a better place. The Spirit body is perfect, it is immortal and cannot be destroyed or harmed. It cannot be affected by natural law or hereditary sicknesses it dwells in the physical body for a period of time decided by God. Then the Spirit body that is perfect returns to God after physical death as God had ordained. You are Down Syndrome or disabled only for a few years. It is the same for all forms of disability, we are born of the flesh of man, so anything can happen. Lazarus was raised from the dead, ten lepers were healed, they all had to die eventually, so do we. It is your choice whether YOUR SPIRIT BODY will live with God and the believers, or with the devil and his fallen angels, after physical death.

What has a bush, an animal and a human being, got in common ?

They are all bodies.

(1) The bush in the back ground of the picture is a body. (2) My son Mark has a dog called Jessie and like Molly the dog in the picture has a body and soul. (3) Conor, Gavin and Garrett my grand children who live in America, have a body soul and Spirit and are made in God's Spirit image and likeness and are immortal. (4) When Jessie and Molly the dogs die, their soul dies with them. Animals are not immortal. If you kick an animal and do not love it, their soul is sad, no joy. If you play with them and love them, they will be joyful. Humans are just the same. (5) God the Father at no time was ever flesh. The flesh body dies, it is mortal. Our spirit body is immortal and never dies it returns to God, for judgement or reward, (hell or heaven).

WE HAVE SQUANDERED OUR YOUNG PEOPLE'S INHERITANCE

WHERE *ARE* THEY NOW ?

WHY *HAVE* THEY GONE ?

WHERE *WILL* THEY END UP ?

THEY ARE NOT FILLING ANY OF THE CHRISTIAN CHURCHES LIKE IT WAS THOUGHT THEY WOULD.

TO KNOW WHY

We should look at the world through the eyes of our young people and see what they see... ask them like I do and they will tell you. The young people feel that God's representatives whom they have rejected by not attending church have let them down in so many ways that they feel that God cannot love them now that they have rejected His representatives. The young people are the future church and need to be evangelised, know the truth and separate it from non - scriptural pious opinions.

The Holy Spirit was the missing factor in the Christian churches of the past and is missing to day. Sectarianism, denominationalism and holy rituals continue, pious opinions abound and are a waste of time.

We must learn from the past and take our heads out of the sand. The Christian churches of the past right up to the present slipped up. They lacked the Holy Spirit and have allowed the soaps on television to dictate to young and old how to live and bring up their children. God's plan for living and marriage is not preached anymore, neither are the young people there to listen. The Christian churches chickened out and became people pleasers. They were afraid to offend people by preaching the commandments or mention sin. The Holy Spirit was neglected, a defect in the Latin churches and I believe in all Christian churches. (Catholic Encyclopedia, page 552, Mary and the Holy Spirit). **Because the Holy Spirit was missing, the word spoken was a dead word, and could not prevent abortion or divorce.** Holy rituals are not of the Lord, the Holy Spirit cannot sustain wrong teaching. Stable families are an exception now.

We have mammies rearing children that have different daddies that are not married, and do not live together. Not married and do live together. Nevertheless God loves them all. When their children grow up they will think this way of life is normal and do the same thing. The parents are responsible for their children's formation, and the religious institutions responsible (past and present) for their parent's formation. We should teach God's plan for life, why we are here and tell about His promises and the gift of free will that God has given to every human being. IT IS MAN'S FREE CHOICE as to whether he wants to follow Jesus or not, and that GOD loves him/her either way.

> *World forces control our economy. Greater wealth has not brought greater happiness.*

Man's **SOCIAL** gospel of brown/white envelopes, bribery, corruption and greed, covers this world only. The **REDEMPTIVE** Gospel (redemptive meaning, buy back, set free from sin, through Jesus) covers this world and the next. The safety of the air we breathe, the food we eat, the water we drink is under scrutiny all the time. Our survival is threatened by weapons and bombs that man's technology provides. Link all that I have just mentioned with the fall off in attendance in all churches. Sectarianism, lack of knowledge of the Word of God and no teaching, means that the conditions are just right for false prophets, mediums, occult practices, fortune telling, astrologers, wizards, witches and tarot card readers who confuse creation with the Creator, as they move in on people's anxieties and fears. Some Christian churches from the time of the seven churches in the book of Revelation to now, can hang their heads in shame, they let it all slip. However I am not their judge. Some teach in their doctrine that the Holy Spirit was only for the apostles and not available to future generations. If you believe this you do not believe God's Word. Some earthly fathers, mothers and leaders of society, church and state have let us down as role models, just like our first parents did. I know that my Heavenly Father will never let me down, my earthly father may.

I said before that God does not bless plans or RELATIONSHIPS that He has not ordained. It does not mean that GOD DOES NOT LOVE YOU if you are in such a RELATIONSHIP

- lesbian or gay, Pope, Bishop, Priest, Nun, Brother, King, Queen, Prime Minister or President - genital sex outside of marriage is forbidden. All human beings must practice chastity, if not they will go to hell when they die if they do not repent. If you do not believe the Word of God you will also go to hell when you die. I am only repeating what God says in his manual.

(Romans 8/9)
THE APOSTLE PAUL SAYS

" IN FACT UNLESS YOU POSSESSED THE SPIRIT OF CHRIST YOU DO NOT BELONG TO HIM - THE SPIRIT OF GOD MUST LIVE IN YOU! IF NOT YOU LIVE IN DARKNESS".

The Spirit of God is a person. Jesus is a person. He does not live in the tabernacle on the altar in the Roman catholic church, in the monstrance or in any church or building. He must live in you. (Acts 17/24) **"The God who made the world and everything in it, is the Lord of heaven and earth and does not live in temples built by hands".**

SO WHO ARE YOU GOING TO BELIEVE

For the Spirit of Jesus to live in you, you must repent, be "born again" and ASK for the Holy Spirit. Because of wrong teaching, lots of people in the Roman catholic church believe that by going to mass and Holy Communion every day that Christ lives in them. As I have said a few times already and, it needs to be said, to think so is to be in error.

People can be institutionalized if they stay in prison, or hospitals for more than six months. I believe that you can be institutionalized by religious doctrine also. The man or woman in prison or wherever is afraid to come out. Religious rituals are the same in that you are afraid to move out, so you stay trapped in wrong belief.

The Catechism of the Roman catholic church states quite clearly on page 390/1741 under Liberation and salvation, "by His glorious Cross Christ has won salvation for all men" which includes women also. He redeemed them from sin that held them in bondage. I believe that for generations people have been institutionalized, held in bondage by religious rituals and laws: "For freedom Christ has set us free". In Him we have communion with the "truth that makes us free'". The Holy Spirit has been given to us and, as the Apostle teaches, "where the Spirit of the Lord is, there is freedom". Already we glory in the "liberty of the children of God"! God does not keep us in bondage, the devil and wrong teaching does. (Matt. 7/11) The Holy Spirit is given to us when we ask in God's time, not man's.

Good works should spring from your faith in Christ.

Make sure that you "are born" again through repentance and that Jesus does live in you. There are some people like I have already said. Who believe that if they say rosaries. Do holy things, do Legion of Mary work, St. Vincent de Paul work, go on retreats, go on pilgrimages, follow holy rituals give all their money to the poor, go to church or mass every day, receive Holy Communion every day, that Christ lives in them. They believe they belong to Christ and will go to heaven when they die, you are misinformed if you do. (R. C. Ency. page 290) In the year 1215, you had to go to Eucharist - Holy Communion only once a year.

(Matt. 6/33)

TO SEEK THE KINGDOM FIRST, I BELIEVE IS TO

ASK FOR AND RECEIVE THE HOLY SPIRIT, (WE

ARE TALKING KINGDOM POWER) AND ALL

ELSE WILL BE GIVEN UNTO YOU.

My confirmation cost my dad and mam a fortune. I was too young as a child to understand what it was all about.

I received the Holy Spirit on the first of November 1986, fifty odd years after my confirmation, as told in my testimony. I do not believe you receive the Holy Spirit at infant baptism, however I was incorporated into the Roman Catholic Church at my infant baptism. I now know after all these years that the confirmation I made at school did not make me a Christian nor was I born one. I became one at age fifty three, by confirming the prayers said over me at infant baptism, by Priest and God parents as I asked for the gift of the Holy Spirit which I received.

(John 15/5) " I am the vine, you are the branches, He who abides in me, and I in him, bears much fruit; for without Me you can do nothing." I know this to be true.

(John 3/8) "The wind blows where it will. You hear the sound it makes, but you do not know where it comes from, or where it goes. So it is with everyone begotten of the Spirit".

The Baptism of the Holy Spirit is a biblical experience that causes biblical teaching to come alive in us, by which God preserves His own from worldly error.

In contrast, false teachers are devoid of the Spirit, despite the claims they make. They are empty preachers.

The Holy Spirit is promised to the followers of Jesus, not the followers of Mary the mother of Jesus, Padre Pio, St. Anthony or anyone else, they are role models only by their example of obedience.

Kingdom power I call it.

MARY was a RECIPIENT of God's grace, as were the apostles as I so often tell people. It's purpose is to endow the receiver with strength and power to overcome, do the will of God and be a witness. (Acts 1/8) "But when the Holy Spirit comes upon you, you will be filled with power and you WILL BE witnesses (not that we might be, you have no choice) for me in Jerusalem, in all Judaea and Samaria and to the ends of the earth." Like others I found this to be true. I did overcome. It is the Holy Spirit that dwells within me, that evangelises and heals the emotions, not me.

(Acts 2/4) Shows that this Baptism is accompanied by speaking in other tongues, as the Holy Spirit gives utterance. Throughout the book of Acts and church history, 'church "meaning the family of believers, those 'born again" who are scattered in various Christian churches, Roman Catholic, Protestant or other mainline churches. Tongues, the least of the gifts, is not for an elite group of people (who would refuse any gift from God?) but for ALL those who have repented, asked and invited Jesus into their lives.

DON'T BE AFRAID, NO MATTER WHAT THE CAUSE OF YOUR LONELINESS - CALL ON THE NAME ABOVE ALL NAMES, JESUS, GOD'S ONLY SON.

(Matt 14-23-27)

After sending the people away, he went up the hill himself to pray. When evening came, Jesus was there alone; and by this time the boat was far out in the lake, tossed about by the waves, because the wind was blowing against it.

Between three and six o'clock in the morning (The fourth watch) Jesus came to the disciples, walking on the water. When they saw him walking on the water, they were terrified. 'It's a ghost!' they said, and screamed with fear.

Jesus spoke to them at once 'COURAGE!' it is I. Don't be afraid!

Then Peter spoke up 'Lord, if it's you,' bid me to come to you on the water.'

'Come!' answered Jesus. So Peter got out of the boat and started walking on the water to Jesus. But when he noticed the strong wind, he was afraid and started to sink down in the water, 'Save me, Lord!' he cried.

At once Jesus reached out and grabbed hold of him and said, 'How little faith you have! Why did you doubt ?'

They both got into the boat, and the wind died down. 'Truly you are the son of God! they exclaimed. I, made Jesus my anchor, as I was the boat being tossed around all the time by the storms of life, how about you?

THE HOLY SPIRIT WILL <u>ONLY</u> RESPOND TO GOD'S WORD, NOT TO PIOUS OPINIONS, HERESY, LIES OR HOLY SPOOF, SOME OF WHICH I SHARE WITH YOU IN LOVE OVER THE NEXT FEW PAGES.

If the word or what you say is not found in Scripture, don't say it if you want your prayers answered.

God will not hold those who compromise the Word of God guiltless. Mary, the mother of Jesus, God in the flesh, said, "do what he tells you". For me He turned water into wine, winter into Spring, darkness into light, my Adam and Eve nature into a Christ like nature. He will do the same for you. Then, like Mary, when the spear or sword pierced her soul (we are all living souls), you will be able to cope like she did, no matter what trauma is in your life. *We can only know what Jesus tells us to do if we read His Word in the Bible.*

We dishonour Mary ?

Mary was the recipient of God's graces, not the dispenser, like I was led to believe. Some people preach and teach that all graces and gifts come from Mary. If you believe this you are being deceived, it is a pious opinion. To believe untruths prevents signs and wonders. We dishonour Mary, the mother of Jesus, with devotion to her that leaves us less open to the working of the Holy Spirit and Jesus in our lives.

It says in Vatican II. (footnotes page 91 chapter 62 - The blessed Virgin and the Church) "That the council applies to the blessed Virgin the title of Mediatrix, but carefully explains this, so as to remove any impression that it could detract from the uniqueness and sufficiency of Christ's position as Mediator. '(I believe it does it is too fine a line for the average person to come to grips with and understand)'. Down through the years we have had too much emphasis on Mary and not enough on the Spirit, the third person of the Trinity, who was there before Mary. When will we learn that people cannot understand these things if they are still in darkness, so why mention Mediatrix, why invent new words and cause confusion. Keep it simple. Luke 24/31-32 says, Then their eyes were opened and they recognised him, and he disappeared from their sight. They asked each other, "Were not our hearts burning within us while he talked with us on the road and opened the scriptures to us?". He will to you also. This is why it is important to read the Word and read the testimonies in this book.

JESUS,

THE NAME ABOVE ALL NAMES

OPENED THE MIND AND EYES OF

THE APOSTLES AND MY MIND AND

EYES,

TO UNDERSTAND THE SCRIPTURES.

Old ideas of the past have not worked and never will without repentance, and conversion.

Instead of the proposed needle in O'Connell Street, we should put up a big empty tent and pray for revival and see the Lord fill it.

Revival is needed and will come through the revelation of the Word of God by the power of the Holy Spirit. The Roman catholic church is in rag order, collapsing from within like Rome did, and sadly, so are most of the institutional Christian churches. We need to teach Christianity not Roman Catholicism, or any other "ISM". We have some great truths in the Roman Catholic church mixed with fiction, holy rituals and pious opinions. I was told that the seminaries around the world, are full of students who want to be Roman catholic priests. If the people that come out of them are not "born again" and baptised in the Holy Spirit, ordained by God, and not by man, then the doctrines that they teach will not be of any use, history will be just repeating itself.

(Tim 2/5) " For there is ONE GOD and there is One who brings God and mankind together, the man Jesus Christ, who gave himself to redeem all mankind". I have already said, why mention Mediatrix and cause confusion. Would you let your children play at the edge of a volcano, or play on a motorway? Certainly not! Your protective instincts would not allow you. Yet the church I was born into does not seem to mind how, or, to whom we pray. It just gets them into the church building at all costs to do all kinds of holy things that do not cause conversion.

The Holy Spirit must be able to sustain what you teach.

However, it says in Scripture that people die for want of knowledge of the Word of God. I believe they die spiritually and physically because of sicknesses caused by activities forbidden by God. We must be bold when speaking, or, teaching the Word and dispense with tradition if it does not come from within the Word and the life of the last of the apostles who were witnesses. (Luke 1/1-4) "Many have undertaken to draw up an account of the things that have been fulfilled among us, just as they were handed down to us by those who from the first were **eye-witnesses and servants of the Word.** Therefore, since I myself have carefully investigated every-thing from the beginning, it seemed good also to me to write an orderly account for you, most excellent Theophilis, so that you may know the certainty of the things you have been taught".

I believe that traditional untruths that have been added since the death of the Apostles and eye-witnesses have no value and lead people astray.

WHY NO ROSARY?

(page 570 Flannery edition - Priests footnote 217)

I READ in **Vatican II** the following: -

" Among the practices of adoration, prayer and piety for priests, one at first sight could be surprised by the omission of the Rosary, because it turns away our other brothers and sisters in Christ. We have to remember it goes on to say, that this is a document intended for the priests of the whole church". *If we as Christians share one faith in Jesus, why teach, do, or say things that will offend other believers.* If we cannot share our prayers as part of the body of believers in public and are conscious of the reason, then we should not say them even in private. We never seem to want to let Mary the mother of Jesus go. We keep dragging her back into all situations, and I am sure screaming and roaring. Jesus alone died on the cross, you cannot share it. Statements that I call untruths that I have already addressed in relation to Mary, are the things that cause division in the body of Christ, the temple that we are all supposed to be built into. Division and pious opinions allow sectarianism, etc. to flourish just like it did in Jesus' time.

It would seem to me, unscriptured individuals have re-written the Word in relation to mediator and intercessor, introduced devotional exercises, rituals, and untruths just for Roman Catholics, that have failed in the past, and that are not acceptable to the body of believers, the church. They deny the free access to our heavenly Father opened up to all believers by the death of Jesus on the cross. They try and have succeeded to bring pious rituals of the past that do not comply with the Word of God, offend the members of other Christian churches and God also into the new millennium.

I, as a "born again" Christian, should be able to go to any Christian Church, for service or Holy Communion and be made feel welcome, like the people that attended the service on 11th. November '01 in the Pro-Cathedral in Dublin. The body of Christ is broken in so many ways.

(John 8/44) No wonder Jesus asks why do we pray like the pagans do and calls us children of the devil. Jesus alone died once and for all, not Mary the mother of Jesus, Padre Pio, Matt Talbot or anyone else.

Mary says in the Word that God did great things for her. He has done great things for me and my wife Dolores, for Paul, Catherine and all of the people of the true testimonies in this book, that can be verified by their changed lives.

When you repent and ask the Father in Jesus name for what you want, not any other name, your life can change too.

Padre Pio, Mother Teresa and a host of others always asked God the Father in Jesus' name, as He told us to do in John's Gospel (16/24) "Until now you have not asked for anything in my name. Ask and you will receive, and your joy will be complete

(Vatican II Flannery page 94/66)

Mary has become a cult figure

Vatican II also says (not John Manning) and I quote "that the cult of praying to Mary differs essentially from the cult of adoration of the Incarnate Word, as well as to the Father and the Holy Spirit". I believe that we should not be praying to Mary, Padre Pio, St. Anthony or any one else.

(Vatican 11 Flannery page 94 footnote 285)

Vatican II also commends a generous devotion to Mary, (I ask why ?) meaning deep affection and loyalty which is at the same time CHRIST CENTERED and free from exaggeration. I believe if you exaggerate Mary's role, say things about her not found in the Word of God, you are not in the Spirit. It is written that the Spirit leads us into all truth.

(Hebs. 2/25)

"Therefore He is able to save to the uttermost those that come to God through Him, since He always lives to make ***intercession*** for them".

We take away from the Word of God and break the commandment that says "thou shall not take the name of the Lord your God in vain," when unscriptured and scriptured individuals in the flesh teach things that cannot be found in the Word. (John 5/39-40) It is written "You search the **Scriptures,** for in them you think you have eternal life; and these are they which testify of Me." "But you are NOT willing TO COME to Me that you may have life".

(Acts 4/12)

"NOR IS THERE SALVATION IN ANY OTHER, FOR THERE IS NO OTHER NAME UNDER HEAVEN GIVEN AMONG MEN BY WHICH WE ARE SAVED".

SO I ASK ?

Who gave anyone the right to say different, to add or take from the Word of God and teach the falsehood, that I have just read in a book called

"THIS IS YOUR MOTHER"

How can there be unity in the body, when wrong teachings are allowed, there are no excuses for it whatsoever. I believe it is heresy.

*

(Matt. 12/50)

JESUS ASKS "WHO IS MY MOTHER ? THIS IS WHAT HE SAYS "WHOEVER DOES WHAT MY FATHER IN HEAVEN WANTS HIM TO DO IS MY BROTHER, MY SISTER AND MY MOTHER".

Jesus is not disowning His family, He is widening the circle to include His new extended spiritual family. I cannot find in Scripture where it allows the INTERPRETATION that Mary, the mother of Jesus is an intercessor, mediator and a distributor of graces, as the aforementioned book teaches and some "Legion of Mary" people and others tell me they believe.

It is your choice, if you want to believe that Mary is the distributor of all graces, an intercessor and mediator-you have free will to do so. *I believe it is heresy to teach this if you are a Christian*. It breaks the commandment that says..."Thou shall not take the name of the Lord your God in vain". By this I mean you are saying something God has not said, but man teaches and is another pious opinion and thus another cult is born.

IF YOU BELIEVE WHAT IS WRITTEN IN THIS BOOK CALLED, **"THIS IS YOUR MOTHER"** YOU WILL NEVER SEE SIGNS AND WONDERS. IT IS A PERSONAL PIOUS OPINION AND CANNOT BE BACKED UP BY SCRIPTURE.

But if Christ is the end, this book goes on to say, then Mary is the way to Him... **Not true!** I believe only by example.

THE "HERESY" CONTINUES, AND I DO NOT APOLOGISE FOR USING THE WORD.

(2 John 1/7-9-10-11) "Many deceivers, who do not acknowledge Jesus Christ as coming in the flesh, have gone out into the world. Any such person is

the deceiver and the antichrist. Anyone who runs ahead and does not continue, in the teaching of Christ does not have God. If anyone comes to you and does not bring this teaching, do not take him into your house or welcome him. Anyone who welcomes him shares in his wicked work".

BE REMINDED ABOUT THE JUDGEMENT IN STORE FOR FALSE PROPHETS WHO SHOULD NOT BE ENCOURAGED IN THEIR WORK.

The book titled "This is your mother" also goes on to say… "the more generous we are with God the more generous He will be with us. He is never outdone in generosity"… **Not True?** God does not love me or is he more generous to me than anyone else because of what I do. You cannot earn God's love. Like faith, it is a gift. (It also says "Christ for thirty years lived at Nazareth in submission to Mary". I myself lived in submission to my mother and father until I was twenty one, they helped my formation).

I believe Jesus was about his father's business at age thirteen. Remember that Mary was only thirteen to fourteen years old when Jesus was born. She was a young mammy. Joseph his step-daddy was there also. The booklet goes on to say that we follow his example when we live fully in dependence on Mary. .. *Not True - heresy !* Mary and Jesus depended on Joseph.

No wonder there is no unity in the churches with this kind of teaching. I, believe, that my heavenly Father will supply all my needs and yours also, if we pray within His will in Jesus' name no matter what denomination you belong to.

It goes on to say in the same book, "As Christ came through her into the world, so now, He communicates the graces of redemption through her"...*Not True!*

And also says, "This is the will of God that we receive all through Mary."... *Not True!*

I will finish with the following quote from the same book. That is allowed by the authorities of the Roman catholic church... "All gifts and virtues, the graces of the Holy Spirit Himself, are distributed to those she chooses, when she chooses, how she chooses, and as much as she chooses". *Not True! No Christian should teach or believe this, so who is in charge?*

The book also says "That when we make our requests through Mary we have in her an advocate so powerful that she is never refused"... *Not True!* (Romans 8/26) I believe the "Spirit Himself makes intercession for us with groanings that cannot be uttered". It is not Mary's role to accept our offerings and pass them on to Jesus, or persuade him to accept them. We need the Spirit of truth to move on this land and all over the world and revival to take place in all the Christian churches. No wonder we see no signs and wonders, with this kind of teaching.

A MESSAGE TO ALL LEADERS

(Jer. 43/2-7) "Leaders do not compromise the truth due to disfavour or alter God's word to appease men. Trust that the Lord protects those He sends to speak His word". I, as an evangelist, sow seeds and some times I water them, knowing, only God can make them grow. He won't make something GROW that HE has not planted. Wrong teaching can allow the devil's bird's of the air to float down and steal the seed just planted if it is not set in good soil. That is why I pray with people over a couple days after I pray the healing and conversion prayer with them. Satan comes along after I sow or water a seed and tries to rob the seed by saying, "don't mind your man".

(Acts 1/4-6)

On one occasion, while he was eating with them Jesus gave them this command: "Do not leave Jerusalem, but wait for the gift my Father promised, which you have heard me speak about. For John baptized with water, but in a few days you will be baptized with the Holy Spirit".

(Acts 1/8)

"But you will receive power when the Holy Spirit comes upon you; and you will be my witnesses in Jerusalem, and in all Judea and Samaria, and to the ends of the earth".

(Eph 4/11 - 15)

"It was he who gave some to be apostles, some to be prophets, some to be evangelists, and some to be pastors and teachers, to prepare God's people for works of service, so that the body of Christ may be built up until we all reach unity in the faith and in the knowledge of the Son of God and become mature, attaining to the whole measure of the fullness of Christ. Then we will no longer be infants, tossed back and forth by the waves, and be blown here and there by every wind of teaching and by the cunning and craftiness of men in their deceitful scheming". I believe that we must speak the truth in love. *A PIOUS OPINION IS NOT A TRUTH.*

HOW TO PRAY IF YO U WANT GOD TO HEAR YOU.

I read on page 582 / ref. 2737/26 of the Catechism of the Catholic Church, pocket edition, the following and I quote "You ask and do not receive, because you ask wrongly, to spend it on your passions. If we ask with a divided heart, we are adulterers."

Do not be afraid to turn to God, and repent and pray in Jesus' name, (no other name) if you want God to hear your prayer. There is nothing in the past that you have ever done, or will do in the future, to prevent God from loving you.

WE MUST PRAY WITHIN THE WILL OF THE FATHER, USING HIS WORDS . THE RESULTS ARE SHARED IN THE TESTIMONIES YOU HAVE JUST READ AND SPEAK FOR THEMSELVES

You yourself must take that step from darkness into the light.

Most Religious Teachers of the past in all denominations, genuine sincere nice people were doing their best to teach in their own strength, and knew very little about the Holy Spirit.

Those without the Holy Spirit inform. Those in the Holy Spirit transform!

Some Institutional religious teachers of the past, of all denominations became control freaks and cult leaders. Cults without Christ, have caused more people to be depressed, sick and lose their souls, because they, as teachers, lacked the guidance of the Holy Spirit, knowledge of the Word of God and his promises and taught ritualistic doctrine.

Most of the things I was told to believe were

pious opinions.

No teaching, with excessive control, driven by religious authority, (particularly in Ireland,) which allows the Word of God to be contaminated with religious rituals and pious opinions, is of any worth to its hearers. We were never told about the healing power of God's

Word or that He sent His Word to heal us. We just said prayers that went nowhere. God allows things to happen to us, so as that we will have total dependence on the Lord, not on rituals or pious opinions.

(Deuteronomy 8/3 Matt 4/4)

Jesus quoted the Old Testament to rebuke Satan, that reads as follows.

"He humbled you, causing you to hunger then feeding you with manna; which neither you nor your fathers had known, to teach you that man does not live on bread alone, but on every Word that comes out of the mouth of the Lord"

We as believers should not be afraid to call on the Word of God to rebuke Satan in Jesus' name, and by the power of the Holy Spirit pray against sickness and stress in our lives. Wrong beliefs, lack of knowledge of the Word of God, false teachings, pious opinions, praying to dead saints canonised by man, will prevent signs and wonders from happening.

God says this about His Word.

We must not break or tamper with his Word (discard it), it is flawless; live according to his Word; we must hide it in our hearts; it's a lamp to our feet. If you speak careless words you **will** be held accountable. We must not peddle it. We must not distort it, but let it dwell in us. It is a living Word, we must not merely listen to the Word and so deceive ourselves. We should do what it says, and any one who does, finds freedom and is blessed in what he does. We must fix God's Word in our hearts.

(REVELATIONS 22/18-19)

Everyone who hears the words of the prophecy in this book; (it is said in Revelation the last book of the bible and, I believe it applies to all the other books) and *ADDS* anything to them, God will add to him the plagues described in the book. If anyone *TAKES AWAY* from this book, God will take away from him (you or I) his share in the tree of life, for every good tree bears good fruit, every bad tree bad fruit. Which tree I ask you, do you want to be fed off in the holy city described in the book.

Are you guilty ?

When YOU say or preach something God has not said, you misuse the name of the Lord your God, you will not be held guiltless. (2 Peter 3/16 - 17) says the following "Some things are hard to understand, which the untaught and unstable distort, as they do also the rest of Scriptures, to their own destruction. You therefore, beloved, knowing this beforehand be on your guard lest, being carried away by the error of unprincipled men, you fall from your steadfastness".

JESUS SAYS " most assuredly, I say to you, the hour is coming, and now is, when the dead (I believe the spiritually dead, like I was) will hear the voice of the son of God; and those who hear will live".

I THANK GOD I HEARD THAT VOICE but sadly not in the denominational church I was born into, for the reasons already mentioned in my testimony. I am sad for the people of to-day and their children, that have not been encouraged to hear that voice because of the lack of teaching.

I AM A SINNER AND A WITNESS and by the grace of God, a living saint as in the Word (I can imagine the nods and the winks. Who is your man, and who does he think he is? I am who God says I am.) All those born again and alive are living saints, so it is written.

(Romans 8/27) "And he who searches our hearts knows the mind of the Spirit, because the Spirit intercedes for the saints (living saints) in accordance with God's will". No one else has the power, so it is written in Scripture. (Psalm 16-3) As for the saints who are in the land, they are the glorious ones in whom is all my delight". I believe any other saint is counterfeit.

(1 Samuel 2-9) "He will guard the feet of His saints, but the wicked will be silenced in darkness". *("It is not by strength that one prevails")* God sent His Word to heal us, and it never returns empty.

Only God knows who is in heaven.

If only God knows who is in heaven, what right has any human being to canonise any dead person to sainthood when scripture tells us that those who are born again are living saints?

The Catechism of the Roman catholic church (page 191 - 823 /289) reads, "The Church, then, is 'the holy People of God', and her members are called 'saints'." Because God's Word is timeless, believers of each generation from the time of Pentecost (the birth of the Church) can expect the same resources and experiences that were afforded the first believers who received the Holy Spirit.

In the twelfth century. (Modern Catholic Encyclopedia page 783) the Western Roman catholic church acknowledged that canonisation required papal authorisation. In the early church, prior to this change, all the faithful were saints. They were holy simply because they had entered into a close relationship with the risen Christ, by becoming member's of the community of followers of Jesus.

When Rome changed things, people started to pray to dead saints canonised by man, have masses offered, do novenas, light candles etc, the cash flow improved for the orders and the person doing the paying and praying went to hell because of this form of idolatry, (meaning to love or venerate to excess).

As I type my way through this page in November 2000, I read that the Roman catholic church that I was born into, and who were responsible for my formation, allowed me to live in a world of novenas, rosaries, sodalities etc., outside of Christ, is now looking for a miracle from Matt Talbot who died June seventh 1925 and Frank Duff who died November seventh 1980 (both without power) to help get people back to church. *Satan can provide the miracles needed to boost this kind of belief. We need to define what the word church means, the church as far as Scripture is concerned means the believers (the living saints), not Roman Catholics, Protestants or those of any denomination, only those who are "born again". * See page 252 ref. Matt. 24/24.

I believe the Christian denominational churches are dead and shrinking, with no young people, no Holy Spirit, no life, they have not learned from past mistakes.

I believe the pride of the intellect can prevent men and women, clergy and lay from asking for the Holy Spirit. They were told they received it at infant baptism, which they do not and very few people receive the Holy Spirit at teenage confirmation. We are still doing the holy things of the past that have failed miserably. When will the leaders of the church that I was born into, move away from the nonsense of the past? We need to get back to the Word of God. Only repentance, and conversion can get people back to church, when they are brought into the knowledge of the Word of God, to understand that they are the church. *The members of Christian churches or any church should examine the doctrine they have been taught and ask questions like I have asked in love.* The Spirit of God must move on this land and in the world, particularly in all Christian churches that are dead. The young people do not see God in the churches or in society anymore. The early Christian church blew it, when some of them merged with Rome under Constantine, (274-337 AD) and the Roman Church was born. I believe this was a great mistake. We must go back to the church of the creed and get into the Bible. Man has contaminated the Word of God, like he has the world and atmosphere. I hear and see to day, a lot of the Christian churches, no exceptions, continuing to make excuses for the past.

Each generation is responsible for the church (the believers) in its generation. It is not their business to make excuses for the past. However it is their business to look to a future in Christ and not allow or teach the things of the past that cause division to recur.

In the past I was a prisoner like many people in other denominations of my religion and doctrine some of which was false, and could not be sustained by the Holy Spirit.

Most of our young people and a lot of the older generations, see quite clearly the mess of the past. They have had enough and do not want to know about religion or the people in charge. Role models of the past have let them down, at home, in church, in government, in schools, in business, they have no one to look up to any more. Some ordinary nice genuine men and women of the past did try to do a good job in their own strength, but limited by the lack of knowledge of the Word of God, have failed by trying to live to standards set by man. If religious teaching is not spirit led or if it teaches pious opinions, the Holy Spirit cannot sustain the teachings.

Unless the Holy Spirit moves and conversion takes place and all religious nonsense and rituals of the past including miracles from dead people STOPS, Satan will go on providing miracles in any name other than Jesus' name. This nonsense of looking for miracles to bring people back to church won't happen. Ten lepers were healed, one returned to give thanks and the other nine returned to the world, where I lived before my conversion, unaware of the fact that I was a sinner until I had my "born again" experience. Miracles do not cause conversion, no more than visions of Mary in the sky, or Padre Pio at the foot of your bed can. All novenas, indulgences etc. should be flushed down the toilet and all the lies told to us in the past should be addressed and apologised for. I believe most of the Christian churches are guilty of sectarianism, either by the doctrine they teach, or because of adhering to the small print in their constitution that causes division. Anything that causes division should be abolished. Young and old people are dying for want of knowledge of the Word of God. They need to be taught the commandments like they learn the rules of road. The Spirit of God cannot move until we come into the truth.

252

(Matt. 24/24)

"For false Christ's and false prophets will appear and perform great signs and miracles to deceive even the elect-if that were possible".

People are still encouraged to pray to dead people that may not be in heaven, like Matt Talbot, Frank Duff and others of the past. No reflection on them, but a sad reflection on the people that encourage this kind of devotion that God has not ordained and is not in keeping with the inspired Word of God. I have already said, that Satan will perform a miracle in any name other than in the name of Jesus. When he does, the people believing it is from God, will turn to Matt or Frank like they do to Padre Pio and others from then on, asking them to intercede for miracles, and another cult that has no power is born and Jesus is set aside. I was not born into the one holy catholic and apostolic Church (as in the creed). I had to have an adult conversion experience like the apostles had and be "born again" to be a follower of Christ. I was born into the family of man, in the Roman Catholic Church, I had to be "born again" into the family of God. Most people are born into the family of man a denomination or cult.

We must be born anew (Page 588) Catechism of the Catholic Church.

You must be "born again" to be a Christian, no matter what your denomination. It is not because John Manning says so. The Catechism of the Roman Catholic Church, Vatican II and the Bible confirm this. Having the name or logo of a denomination written on your forehead will not get your spirit body and soul into heaven when your physical body dies.

Who Intercedes and mediates for us?

Read the following scriptures for yourself in the New International Study Version of the Bible.

(Hebs. 7/25- Rom. 8/26-34.- Iss. 53/12-. 1 Tim. 2/1. Job 16/20) Job believes he has a friend in heaven who will plead with God on his behalf. "There is only one intercessor between God and man and that is Jesus". (Romans 8/26-27) "The Holy Spirit intercedes for us with groans that words cannot express". "The Spirit intercedes for the saints, the living saints in accordance with God's will".

In the early church everyone that was a follower of Jesus was a living saint. In the twelfth century Rome decided to change this.

The church that I was born into moved the goal posts so many times I cannot keep count.

The reason for the invocation of saints according to the modern Roman Catholic Encyclopedia (page 783 - under the heading of saints) is to ask their intercession as in the doctrine of the communion of the saints, that is; the belief that there is communication with the dead by prayer, and that those who have gone before can also pray efficaciously for the living because of their single - minded dedication to prayer and good works when they were alive. *I believe this to be a pious opinion and not in keeping with Scripture.* I was misled. I believe it is the community of the living saints that ask God the Father in Jesus' name for the things they need, not dead ones. ***Surely this is the way it should be, (1 Cor. 1/2)*** "To the church of God which is at Corinth. To those who are sanctified in Christ Jesus, called to be saints, with all who in every place call on the name of Jesus Christ our Lord, both theirs and ours".

I believe that is when the church of the creed became Roman, the written word that is timeless was changed.

The early church prior to the twelfth century change, declared all the faithful "saints." The term is taken from the Latin, *sancti,* which means "holy ones." They were holy simply because they had entered into close relationship with the risen Christ by becoming members of the community of followers of Jesus. I say the things that I say in love.

There is no perfect church out there, only where two or more are gathered together in Jesus' name, on a street corner or in a building. When they stand together the ground becomes Holy Ground.

Faith in Christ and good works must go together. If you are not a saint while you are here, you will not be one in heaven. If you do not experience the kingdom power here, you won't be in the kingdom of heaven later on. No matter who you are, or what you have.

I believe when we pray for the living and the dead at church, we pray for those in Christ, living saints in this world but not of it, who will be saints in the next world. The dead, are those in church not born again.

As I have said before, I prayed to saints before my conversion experience who may not even be in heaven and I repented of it. Then things happened for me, I received the Holy Spirit.

Church leaders who encourage people to pray to saints, give Satan a foothold because of an untruth that encourages those that lack the knowledge of the Word of God to pray to saints canonised and declared by man and not by God.

 The life style and example of a holy person, should encourage us, if, what they do is in keeping with the word. If not they distort the Word of God. Only God knows who is in heaven.

I was in and of the world before my conversion.

I am still in it but not of it.

Things I thought I could not do without, I do

not need anymore.

(John 17/9-15-19)

I was in the world physically and of it as I have stated in my testimony, until I had my conversion. I am still in the world but not of it. Material things do not interest to the same degree anymore. Jesus says "I am not praying for the world, but for those you have given me, for they are yours". "He does not pray that God should take me out of the world, but that "He keep me and you from the evil one. **Sanctify them by the truth; your Word is truth".**

It is so easy to tempt God, who never tempts us (like, "I am going to jump off this bridge, so, save - me", he would say to you, "What did you do that for, you idiot". Jesus did not jump when Satan tempted him to jump from the pinnacle of the Temple, He knew better.

God never tempts us. If you say something that God has not said, the Holy Spirit will not bear witness to what you say, then you have no access to the fullness of God's love, you are an empty preacher.

(2 Tim. 2/15)

We must correctly handle the Word of God.

If you DO, don't worry. If you DON'T you need to!

(Revelations 22 - 14-15)

Blessed are those who do His commands that they may have the right to the tree of life, and enter through the gates of the city. But outside are the dogs and the sorcerers the sexually immoral and murderers, which I as a sinner, had the potential to be until I accepted Jesus as my Lord and saviour. God has committed to man the knowledge of His Word to help him cope with the trials of life, the desires of the flesh, sickness etc. He does not bless plans, behaviours, relationships or holy rituals that He has not ordained. I was always encouraged to pray to saints, men and women that may not be in heaven, canonised by man, who led me to believe for their own reasons that dead people had power. I now know this not to be true. If you want to PRAY to dead people, that is your choice God has given man free will to do what he wishes.

I am asking many questions in this book

IN LOVE, like for example…

WHY DO WE NOT PRAY TO

MATTHEW, MARK, LUKE OR JOHN,

WE KNOW WHERE THEY ARE?

IF ONLY GOD KNOWS WHO IS IN HEAVEN WHY PRAY TO SOMEONE THAT PRESENT CENTURY MAN HAS INTRODUCED WHO MAY NOT BE IN HEAVEN.

Page 582 of the Catechism of the Roman Catholic Church 2737-26 says " If we ask with a divided heart, we are adulterers" I believe this it what we are, when we ask in any other name like, Mary, Padre Pio, Divine Mercy etc. instead of the name of Jesus.

(Matt. 16-18)

"And I tell you that you are Peter, and on this rock I will build my church, and the gates of Hades will not overcome it".

Jesus is the rock on which God is building His spiritual church (man has hijacked it) with living stones like you and I, the believers, and the gates of Hades shall not prevail against it. It is also built on the foundations of the Apostles and prophets. You do not have to look too far today to see that the gates of hell have overcome and prevailed against the institutional churches. They are dying a death, however, the number of "born again" Christians in the world today is growing. You will find them in the old Institutional churches, in the house churches and outside. God is building His church whether man want's it or not. This book has nothing to do with being denominational or non-denominational, you can be a member of the Roman Catholic Church, Protestant Church, Lutheran Church, Baptist Church, Anglican Church, Methodist Church, Church of England or Ireland, Apostolic, Assemblies, or House Church. Some think they have it right, and exclusive and believe that everyone else, not in their group is lost. Only God knows who is lost.

Society rejects dependence on God.

All man-made, man-directed institutional churches, to me, are earth bound, including the one I was born into. The one holy catholic apostolic Church as in the Creed founded on the Faith of the Apostles in Christ is Universal. I believe it stretches from the heart of every "born again" Christian, to the highest heaven where God dwells above the third heaven and embraces the sun moon and stars, the celestial (heavenly) bodies and the earth where we dwell.

The church of the creed, living stones (all of whom are "born again" Christians) who like myself are planted by God and allowed to exist in denominational churches, must ignore the things not of the Lord, in their doctrine. At Jesus' second coming, all the believers those who have died in Christ, will come back with him, but there will be no denominational tags they will have fallen off! All who are "born again" and alive on earth, will be taken up to join him. Make sure you are not left behind. Being a Christian has to do with being "born again", being able to do greater things than Jesus did, by asking God the Father in His name. We have no power of ourselves; but we do have a power within us, if we are "born again" and have asked and received the Holy Spirit.

*Since I discovered **LIMBO** was a big lie. I decided to have a look at **PURGATORY** and discovered it was introduced by Gregory the Great (590-604) and there is no reference to it anywhere in the Bible. If you are waiting on the bus for purgatory, I do not think it will ever arrive.*

(Purgatory reference page 704 - The Modern Catholic Encylopedia and Hans Kung's short history of the catholic church, page 72)

I believe there are only two places your spirit body and soul can go when your earthly body dies, your choice is heaven or hell. (It does not matter what I believe) If you want to believe in purgatory fine, that is your choice. I only believe what I can confirm in scripture. I cannot find confirmation as to its existence written in the Word of God. It mentions nothing about a lay-by or a place called *purgatory.* How can you set people a side for a while if their spirit body and soul lives outside of time? I was told that 2 Maccabees explains purgatory. If Judas (not Judas Iscariot) had not believed that the dead would be raised, it would have been foolish and useless to pray for them. In his firm and devout conviction that all God's people would receive a wonderful reward. Judas made provision for a sin offering to set free from their sin, those who had died. I believe this to be a wrong teaching. Who ever said Judas was right. Jesus is the fulfilment of the Old Testament. Had you died in sin in the Old Testament times, and you did not believe in the redeemer to come, or the Word of God, you would go to hell, the same thing applies today. We are new covenant people. The only people you should pray for are the living and the "dead". The dead are those who are not born again, we pray and ask God the Father to bring them closer to Jesus. The living are those that are "born again" and live their lives in the Spirit, followers of Jesus, they walk the walk and talk the talk. They will receive a wonderful reward.

When your physical body that is mortal dies, your Spirit body that is immortal lives outside of time. The New Testament tells us that by the death of Jesus on the cross, we are saved and redeemed at no cost to us, if we believe.

Matt. 5-25 is a New Testament scripture that is used by some in the Roman catholic church, the stable that I was born into, to confirm purgatory.

I believe they misinterpret this Scripture that reads as follows:- "Settle matters quickly with your adversary who is taking you to court. Do it while you are still with him on the way, or he may hand you over to the judge, and the judge may hand you over to the officer, and you may be thrown in prison. I tell you the truth you will not get out until you have paid the last penny". This is what man will do, without mercy, and out will go your wife and children on to the side of the road. I personally nearly had it happen. God shows us here that He is merciful and that His son Jesus has paid all our bills. You need a great imagination to get purgatory out of the Scripture quoted. You do not have to pay or settle with God to get into heaven. Jesus, God's only Son paid the price with His life to redeem the world. Heaven is the fulfilment of the hopes of God's people beyond their earthly life which is temporary. To qualify we must repent, feel regret for a deed or omission. (Genises 6/3-7) God said at one time "He was sorry he had created the human race, and that man would not live beyond 120 years".

(the strong man tied up, symbolises the Devil the ruler of the world and the minds

and hearts of men and women - picture by Catherine of the Paul and Catherine

story in this book)

As an evangelist I rob houses, and reclaim for the Lord ground lost to Satan.

It is written in Matthew 12/29

"That no man can break into a strong man's house and take away his belongings unless he first ties up the strong man; then he can plunder his house"

I believe that this parable is like the parable of the old wine skin not being able retain the new wine... The old and new tenant cannot occupy the same house. I believe we have to tie up the strong man Satan, who controls the inherited sinful nature that dwells in us since the fall of our first parents and which is passed down through the generations. Jesus drove the money changers out of the temple, (John 2/14-15-16) Only Jesus can drive the desires of the flesh out of you, so as that He can take up residence.

Romans 7/18

I know that nothing good lives in me, that is, in my sinful nature.

We have a choice of natures, our 'Adam and Eve' inherited human sinful nature or a 'Christ-like Holy Spirit' led nature. Every human being, male or female, President, Priest or Pastor, rich man, poor man, Pope, King or Queen, no exceptions should invite Jesus to come live in them, just like Mary did.

The following Scripture explains **the sinful nature** that we inherited from our first parents and explains the reasons why people do awful things to one another.

(Galations 5/19)

"The acts of the sinful nature are obvious: sexual immorality, impurity and debauchery; idolatry and witchcraft; hatred, discord, jealousy, fits of rage, selfish ambition, dissension, factions and envy; drunkenness, orgies, and the like. When we live in this state we will not inherit the kingdom of God".

Every "born again" Christian is catholic, no matter what denomination he or she is born into.

All born again Christians baptized in the Holy Spirit, should live their lives in the Spirit and by the power of the Spirit they should walk the walk and talk the talk, if they don't they have problems. To me the word catholic is misused and abused by many, the word means universal, a church made up of all the believers. I say it again, I was not born into the catholic church, I was born into the Roman catholic church.

DOMESTIC VIOLENCE

CAN YOU COPE ?

People in the Spirit do not subject others to domestic violence or violence of any kind (Gal. 5/22) "For the fruit of the Spirit is Love, joy, peace, patience, kindness, goodness, faithfulness, gentleness and self control. These are brought forth by the transforming work of the Holy Spirit within us as we grow in holiness and in maturity in Christ.

DOMESTIC VIOLENCE IS A CRIME
PUNISHABLE BY MAN AND BY GOD.

It can happen to you because you are a woman, and happens to men also, whether married or shacking up. It is humanly impossible to understand in the flesh (meaning human nature without God) how anyone, man or woman can tell you they love you one minute and in the next few minutes or hours beat you up. People can and do subject other people to domestic violence, using physical, sexual, emotional, verbal, mental and scare tactics to get control. They do it just once they know it works and they never let up.

I believe stalkers are people like that and bide their time till the right person comes along. Sex offenders are the same. Many homes in Ireland and around the world are prisons without bars for men women and children caught up and subject to domestic violence. These prisons are found behind the closed doors of the houses on your road, avenue, lane, grove, park, cul-de-sac or on a farm, it does not matter where you live. *Freedom is possible from a situation like this and any situation that causes you to be imprisoned emotionally, by the power of the Holy Spirit.*

Every baby, in every mammie's tummy, married or not, is a spirit being made in God's spirit image and likeness and knows when mammy is being treated badly.

Mammy Daddy you frighten me.

What a memory bank for any child to live out of.

The developing person in mammie's tummy, says 'mammy /daddy do not shout and roar so much'. *'Daddy do not hit mammy',' mammy do not hit daddy, "you frighten me, I am afraid".* Having to live with domestic violence, which is under reported in Ireland, can be the cause of you losing your spirit body to hell. We are living souls, spirit body, and immortal. Get out, do not risk it, get help for yourself and the perpetrator, once it starts it rarely ends. The perpetrators will get down on their knees, apologise, whinge and cry, promise to give you all their money etc. and commit the same crime a few minutes, hours or days later, make all kind of promises, tell lies till the cows come home. You and your children can be damaged beyond repair, emotionally and physically be miserable in this life, and maybe go to hell when you die and be miserable there if you cannot forgive the perpetrator. Don't hang around. When you leave, tell the children that daddy/mammy is not well and needs help, it will not be easy. Pray with your children in the power of the Holy Spirit, that God will bring their dad/mam closer to Jesus, by seeking the kingdom, first for yourself and then for your partner. It does not mean you must go back again to be beaten up.

Who wants to go back into a burning house. Women that are subject to domestic violence rarely leave home, THEY ARE DRIVEN OUT, there is a difference.

Leaving the relationship does not guarantee the safety of the mammy/daddy or the children. Abusive men/women might get more violent to try and recapture control. As a community we must be on the alert all the time. I have found that by praying with the children, in the power of the Holy Spirit, you prevent a hate build up between mam, dad and children. They will be able to forgive, and not retain any sin of unforgiveness towards dad, mam or others. Professional help and shelter should be sought at all times. *Marriage is about being faithful, in all areas; faithful in providing, caring, loving helping, sharing.* Domestic violence is a crime and some times the perpetrators are protected by their families and friends because of pride; "do not let the neighbours know", "we are a perfect family"! They can attend church, dress well and blame everybody but themselves. Perpetrators need help, you do not help by covering up or being in denial. This life is only temporary, and God wants you to enjoy it to the full, with Him as Lord. The next life that we are created for is outside of time and is forever. You can still love the perpetrator but not put up with the abuse. Turn to God, and ask Him to bring you and the perpetrator close to Jesus, by forgiving, repenting and asking for the Holy Spirit, then you will cope. Make Jesus the person in your life. Ask Him to come and live in you, and fulfil the plan God has for you and yours. I did and He will. My mother called the people that subject others to any kind of violence as street angels and house devils.

Signs to watch out for in a man or women, before you shack up or decide to get married.

Signs to watch out for in a man or woman who subjects others to domestic violence: they lose their temper a lot, get angry and violent in different ways and for the least thing; drink too much, abuse substances and can be possessive and jealous, has strict ways about the male privilege, can be a church goer, a pillar of society and hold down a good job.

So why do women, some married some not, put up with domestic violence.

(Genises 3-16)

I found the answer in the following scripture, that reads as follows, "To the woman He said: "I will greatly multiply your sorrow and conception; In pain you shall bring forth children; Your desire *SHALL* be for your husband, and **he *SHALL* rule over you".** (Gen. 3/16) "This does not mean that the woman is to blame, it is a condition. When I pray with a woman (having being invited to do so) who is subject to domestic violence, I pray out the word desire and pray in the Holy Spirit. Most women will put up with a lot to please their man, it is something that comes natural and is in keeping with the nature we inherited from of our first parents after their fall from grace.

God says the following about marriage.

(Eph, 5/22-33 is worth reading)

Religion plays a big part for men and women who live with a controlling partner who subjects them to abuse. The Bible says "Wives submit to your husbands." and "husbands love your wives as you love yourself". Husbands and wives should be flexible, accommodate or give way to one another be reasonable and understanding, and be helpers to one another, now that they are one. The Bible says, "The husband is the head of the wife as Christ is head of the church". You do not have to be blindly obedient, you are expected to serve one another's needs. Jesus compares His relationship to the believers, the church, where Jesus is the servant who gave his life for all, he served the needs of people. He was head of the church, the model for marriage, with a servants attitude. He never bossed people around, threatened, hit or frightened them. The husband /wife relationship has to be the same, love one another and yourself, like Jesus loves the believers, the church, Col. 3/19.

(Matt. 19/6)

"What God has joined together, let no man put asunder". I believe this meant Bishop, Judge or man. Now I believe it means the perpetrator is causing the separation by his or her behaviour. The law makers then enforce the law. Any man or woman that subjects their spouse or children to violence or abuse, is putting asunder the marriage that they have asked God to bless. *The violence is the cause of the break up so the perpetrator is the one responsible for the break up.* The divorce or separation is a public statement that the marriage has been destroyed by abuse. Any man or woman guilty of domestic violence or any kind of wrong, live out of their inherited Adam and Eve sinful nature as I have already said on another page. Galations 5/19 is quite clear about this and reads as follows. The acts of the sinful nature are obvious; sexual immorality, impurity, and debauchery; idolatry and witchcraft; hatred, discord, jealousy, fits of rage, selfish ambition, dissension, factions and envy, drunkenness, orgies, and the like. *We can see all of the above mentioned in all walks of our society today, including business, religion, government, teaching, pop stars, sports stars including footballers*

CHAPTER 3

Wrong beliefs prevent signs and wonders.

I believe in God the Father of the Trinity. I also believe the woman at the well was the first evangelist after Jesus and for the following reason. When Jesus spoke to her she went back and told the people in the village, (who kept miles away from her in the past, because of her life style) what Jesus had said and they believed her. Once you hear His voice you will want to tell everyone, I know. I am a follower of Jesus, and people tell me that I am an evangelist, the harvest is great and the workers are few. If you want to join me let me know. Let Jesus touch you, like he has touched me and others, who could not cope, what have you to lose. Let Jesus speak into your life. As I have already said, give up all these novenas, rosaries and holy things, read the bible, let God talk to you, instead of you talking to him *with repetitive babble. (Matt. 6/7) "And when you pray, do not use vain repetitions as the heathen do. For they think they will be heard because of their many words". "Therefore do not be like them. For your Father knows the things you have need of before you ask".*

(John 16/12-13)

If you believe a lie you will not see signs and wonders. The Holy Spirit sustains truth and will lead you to the complete truth.

***

Over the next few pages I will address some of the untruths and wrong beliefs which I believe nullifies the movement of the Holy Spirit and prevents signs and wonders.

***

SO I ASK ?

Is what you believe

a pious opinion or a truth ?

I read the following in Vatican II

The layman's call to the Apostolate.

Flannery page 492-3.

"The laity derive the right and duty with respect to the Apostolate from their union with Christ the head. Incorporated into Christ's mystical body through baptism and strengthened by the power of the Holy Spirit through confirmation, they are assigned to the Apostolate by the Lord himself. They are consecrated into a royal priesthood and a holy people".

I believe that our priesthood dies with us as it does with an ordained Roman catholic priest or clergy man. The priesthood of men and women, who are born again has been ignored by the organized institutional Christian churches.

I believe you are misled !

If you believe that the water at infant baptism is the new birth or anything more than symbolic then you are into wrong belief.

I believe if you were told that by your infant baptism you became a Christian a new birth, like I was told, then you were mislead like I was. You have to become a Christian, confirm your baptismal vows as an adult in God's time not man's. Conversion can take place on your death bed after repentance, (not confession) and the acceptance of Jesus as God's only Son, your Lord and Saviour. I call this the vine yard experience, in a the last minute for the same reward as those who have known Jesus for years. You could be the greatest crook that ever lived and still go to heaven when you die, if you repent and are born again from above. Ask God's only Son to come and live in you.

Col. 2/12-14 - The good News Testament

"You have been buried with Christ, when you were baptized; and by baptism, too, you have been raised up with him through your belief in the power of God who raised him from the dead".

I believe it is the adult baptism not infant baptism this Scripture is talking about. I also believe the Scripture in (Luke 11/13) confirms this in the following. "How much more will your Father in heaven give the Holy Spirit to those who ask him!" a infant cannot ask.

John baptized the adults with water for the forgiveness of sins, and said that Jesus would baptize them with the Holy Spirit. God grants forgiveness when there is repentance. Repentance (which means a deliberate turning away from sin to righteousness) is essential, before a person can be baptized in the Holy Spirit. Infant baptism has no power it just incorporates us in to a church or denomination. Boys and girls can be junior member's of a golf club up to a certain age, then they may apply for full membership with voting rights etc. However they have to ask. They can say yes or no if accepted. Having been incorporated into a denomination, we have a choice, we must repent, ask God our Father for the Holy Spirit, and confirm our wish to be born again.

(Luke 4/14)

The Holy Spirit anointed Jesus for His ministry, so must you and I be anointed. "Jesus returned to Galilee in the power of the Spirit, and news about him spread through the whole countryside". The adult men and women of the early church before the merger with Rome, stood in line wearing long white robes, men in the morning and women in the afternoon, different times for both. They walked down a set of steps through the water to steps on the opposite side, total immersion, to be blessed by an elder as they emerged. We need to go back to this. Your body becomes the temple of God's Holy Spirit after adult repentance and baptism, being born again and inviting Jesus come live in you.

I believe you have been misled and also sin, if you believe the teaching that Mary the mother of Jesus was born without sin.

Jesus had to be born of an ordinary woman of the flesh, if He was to be man in the flesh ?

If you believe that the immaculate conception means that Mary the mother of Jesus was born without sin, or that she is the intercessor or mediator between God and man, or between Jesus and God on behalf of man, then you too have been misled. That is the role of the Holy Spirit. Mary's role is a role of example and obedience from generation to generation.

(Flannery edition, Vatican 11 page 85-86/53 chapter VIII the role of the Blessed Virgin Mary, Mother of God, in the mystery of Christ and the church-256)

"At the same time, however, because she belongs to the offspring of Adam she is one with all human beings in their need for salvation". (Luke 1/47) **"And my spirit has rejoiced in God my Savior".** *I believe anything else is a pious opinion.*

Jesus says in (John 6-44) " No one can come to me unless the Father who sent me draws him, and I will raise him up on the last day". To believe different is a sin, an untruth, the Spirit won't respond to untruths. You are a false prophet if you tell people that if they do holy things, and experience infant baptism that their body becomes the temple of God's Holy Spirit, then you lead them astray.

MARY WHO LOVED GOD FIRST

WAS PRESENT

AT PENTECOST,

TO RECEIVE THE

HOLY SPIRIT. SHE WAS

OBEDIENT, MADE THE DECISION AND

JOURNEY TO FOLLOW JESUS HERSELF,

SO MUST YOU.

(Revelation 12/4-5)

Tells us

that the dragon stood in front of

the woman.

"The dragon stood in front of the woman so that he might devour her child the moment it was born. She gave birth to a son, a male child who will rule the nations with an iron sceptre, not tyranny but with boldness and love, and her child was snatched up to His throne"- the ascension of Christ, the woman symbolizes God's people Israel, through whom the Messiah came forth. Mary the mother of Jesus did not crush the serpents head, her offspring Jesus did.

I believe that there was only one person ever born without sin, and that was Jesus who set aside His Divinity, and lived just like you and I, a man subject to the same temptations, but never sinned. He had to grow in faith like you and me, he was human, born into time and called on the Father to get him through each time he was in trouble or needed a miracle to glorify God.

So what do you think Jesus was like ?

He ate, He talked to everyone and anyone, tax collector's, prostitutes, He would have spoken to Roman Catholics had they been around, which is more than a lot of so called Christians do to day, however I am not their judge. He did not sin, He bled, He died as the scriptures foretold. He foretold His resurrection, no other religious leader ever done so, they are still in their tombs. He was nailed to a cross and died in front of His earthly mother, and many others who witnessed His death. He wondered at one stage had His Father forsaken him. I often wondered the same thing about myself. He was God's only son. He rose from the dead on the third day and sits on the right hand side of the Father in Heaven. He showed us that **we** too could overcome the desires of the flesh by THE POWER OF THE HOLY SPIRIT, by turning to God and believing.

Jesus does not ask God for the things we want anymore. We can ask God ourselves for what we want in Jesus' name.

However we must always worship in spirit and in truth, be born again, die to our inherited sinful nature and take on the nature of Christ. (John 4-23) "But the hour is coming, and now is, when the true worshipers will worship the Father in spirit and truth; for the Father is seeking such to worship Him". (John 4/24) "God is Spirit, and those who worship Him must worship in spirit and truth." I personally believe it does not matter where you worship as long as you are in harmony with God who is Spirit.

My prayer must be sincere and according to biblical mandate, pious opinions mean nothing.

(Mark 16/17)

IT IS WRITTEN

THAT SIGN AND WONDERS WILL

FOLLOW THOSE WHO BELIEVE.

WHERE ARE

THE SIGNS AND WONDERS I ASK ?

I

believe

AND HAVE EXPERIENCED SIGNS AND
WONDERS. SO HAVE THE PEOPLE OF THE
TESTIMONIES IN THIS BOOK.

WE HAVE

ALL HAD THIS CONVERSION

EXPERIENCE

AND KNOW THAT GOD'S WORD IS A

LIVING WORD.

Does the BIBLE have a place in the world today ?

I discovered the following letter that was written in 1907 and I share it with you over the next few pages. It is an extract from my Roman Catholic Edition of "The Good News Bible".

The Bible is a collection of books which presents two faces to a Christian.

It is the inspired Word of God, yet at the same time it reflects the limitations of the people who actually wrote it.

It is the inspired Word of God, which cannot be displaced by anything else or any other voice as a supremely authoritative source of *religious truth. Other sources of information about God may carry weight, particularly, for Roman Catholics, the voice of the Pope and they may even be accorded equal weight to that of the Bible. *But they can never supplant it, still less contradict it.* Indeed, all other sources of Christian teaching appeal to the Bible for support. * I BELIEVE THIS SHOULD READ SPIRITUAL TRUTH.

This collection of sacred writings came to its climax in the New Testament, with the words and deeds of the Son of God himself and of the Holy Spirit.

The earthly life of Jesus Christ is described in detail in the bible from his miraculous conception by the Holy Spirit in the womb of the Virgin Mary, to his crucifixion, resurrection and ascension to heaven. His teaching is reported, and its consequences are demonstrated in the actions and explanations of the apostles and the people who became the first followers of Jesus. The power of the Holy Spirit permeated the everyday lives of ever increasing numbers of people, and the New Testament writings tell of their experiences. Everything that happened before the time of Jesus was pointing towards him, and gets its meaning from him. From the creation of the world, right through the history of the Hebrew people, God was showing himself to the world. The people God chose for this, and who listened to him, left an account of their experiences in the words of the Old Testament. If God's plan of salvation reaches its climax in the

New Testament, as Christians believe it does, it was foreshadowed in God's actions throughout history, and particularly in his chosen people, the Hebrews.

So the Old Testament leads naturally into the New Testament, and provides invaluable pointers to the true significance of the New Testament. The two parts of the Bible combine to form a single whole.

The Roman Catholic Church's Attitude to the Bible

The Roman Catholic Church gives such importance to the Bible that parts of it are read at every Mass, and it plays a prominent part in every other church service. Moreover, the readings are arranged in such a way that the whole of the Bible is used, not merely the sections which are thought to be particularly important.

The Bible plays a vital part in the deliberations of the Church at every level, from the most local to the highest. It figures prominently at councils of the whole Church, at synods and in pronounce

-ments where the Church speaks to all her members and to the world.

All members of the Church are urged to study the Bible with reverence and care, and it is an essential source for religious education at all levels.

Sometimes the impression has been given that the Roman Catholic Church does not really trust her members to read the Bible for themselves in case they come to wrong conclusions. Long before the Second Vatican Council set the scene for the guidance of Catholics in today's world, Popes had urged Roman Catholics to study the Bible for themselves, using translations of it into their own languages. Pious X, for example, in 1907 gave his warm approval to societies within the Church which were helping people to use the Bible, and called their efforts "one of the most useful and timely of projects" because such work helps to destroy the impression "that the Roman Catholic Church has any objections to the reading of the Sacred Scriptures in the vernacular, or places any obstacle in the way of the practice." Moreover, the reader is encouraged to go to the Bible itself.

The insight and accumulated wisdom of the Church must be used to help appreciate the full meaning of the biblical text and the truths it contains, but there is no substitute for the actual words of the Bible: "The Sacred Pages themselves; written under inspiration of the Holy Ghost, abound in their own intrinsic meaning; enriched by divine virtue, they have their own power." *Extract of Letter to Cardinal Cassetta, 21ˢᵗ January 1907, commending the work of the society of St. Jerome.*

WHAT A WASTE OF 93 YEARS - WHERE DID IT ALL GO WRONG - MAN TOOK OVER AND SCREWED THINGS UP.

This book is a wake up call ?

I believe that the early Christians made a big mistake by getting involved with Rome, when they had them on the ropes, sometime between 274 and 337 when Constantine co-opted the existing network of authority and communication of the Christian Churches as a kind of civil service, to help him run his empire that stretched all around the Mediterranean and northwards into much of Europe. I believe that the church founded on the faith of the Apostles, was flushed down the loo at that time. (page 200 The Modern Catholic Encyclopedia).

IF OTHER FORMULAE FOR

HEALING

ARE NOT WORKING FOR

YOU, TRUST IN GOD,

TRY THE LORD'S FORMULA,

IT IS YOUR CHOICE

SWAP YOUR OLD

NATURE FOR A NEW NATURE AND SEE

YOUR LIFE CHANGE.

In this book you may identify with some of stories of the people who found it very difficult to cope with the traumas of life and the desires of the flesh, but who now can by the grace of God.

IF THE CAUSE

OF YOUR LONELINESS IS

NOT LISTED OR MENTIONED IN THE

TESTIMONIES, AND YOU KNOW WHAT

IT IS, ADD IT TO THE LIST

I NOW ASK YOU ? WHAT DO

you

WANT TO DO ABOUT YOUR

LONELINESS ?

The living word of God healed the cause of conflict in my life and will do the same for you, after you have repented and pray within the will of the Father, by asking for the Holy Spirit in Jesus name. Pious opinions have no power, or, standing. They are like dark clouds in the distance that never bring rain. If you want healing, find that peace that defies all human understanding, or go to heaven when you die, then ask Jesus into your life now.

Tomorrow is a period nowhere to be found, except perhaps in the fool's calendar. So I do not do novenas or vigils anymore.

What a promise for those who cannot cope.

(Romans 8/18)

It is WRITTEN that "OUR present sufferings (mention your problem or condition) are not worth comparing with the glory that will be revealed in us Christians". This life I believe, healthy or not is temporary._Our souls are saved and our flesh bodies are subject to pain and suffering that we can overcome. I look forward with hope to my resurrection body being free from pain, sin and no more death.

We must REMEMBER that the world we live in is temporary and that we do not live in an enduring city, it will come to an end, heaven and earth will fade away, so will your suffering, no matter who you are or what you have. But the word will never change. So why in the church I was born into, do they keep adding to the word and taking away.

(Genises 6/3) "It is written that man's physical body will not live beyond one hundred and twenty years". We must look forward to that city to come where our spirit body and soul will live in paradise out side of time, where the thief on the cross went, the present heaven or in the new heaven.

It is also written that it is better to lose a leg, arm or eye or have the problems you have, that cause loneliness, than lose your soul.

THE THINGS WE SUFFER, CAN BE SOUL DESTROYING

So what is your soul? We are living souls - (a sword pierced Mary's soul at the cross. I was led to believe my soul was like a little black board within me and only my mother knew where it was and saw my lies) - from head to toe and from finger tip to finger tip. We are spirit beings covered with skin to make us visible.

God is a spirit being and a person! So, are we. God has no flesh. We have a temporary fleshy body that cannot enter heaven ! A vessel that our spirit body lives in, until it dies and the spirit body and soul returns to God. I believe we exist in this world, and that our spirit body and soul are made for the next. I do not believe that there is a lapse of time between physical death and the spirit body being with God. Thank God for where you are right now, broken, lonely, feeling unfulfilled or whatever. In your brokeness, REPENT, turn to God and ask him to bring you close to His only son Jesus, as only He can. No one else has this power. I repented as did my wife   Dolores, Paul, Catherine, Gerry, Mary, along with millions more around the world. We moved beyond THE PAST, so, what was your past like. Were you, are you an angry person, holding resentments, or whatever. I have shared mine by the power of the Holy Spirit, no other power - when you do, then your life can change too.

Most of the time in my work an evangelist I meet the assumed personality of the person, which is different from the real personality.

Having experienced the signs and wonders recorded in this book that can be proven in my own life and in the lives of the people I have shared and prayed with

I know now if I believe untruths, or believe that pious opinions are the Word of God, I will (a) never have a personal relationship with Jesus, (b) be born again, (c) experience signs and wonders, (d) or go to heaven when I die.

I also believe they are some of the reasons why so many people are sick, depressed, fearful and lonely, in pain, no hope, wondering what life is all about, unfulfilled, unloved and feeling empty, afraid to let go and die, and when they do, they leave behind a history of unanswered prayers.

I believe just like Dolores, Paul, Catherine and thousands of other people, that OUR FORMATION prevented us from receiving the Holy Spirit. (I did not know that I had to ask) - as I have already quoted in earlier pages. I lacked the KNOWLEDGE of the WORD OF GOD - it was incomplete. Man of the flesh who does not want to follow for his own reasons, God's commands and speaks of God as a kill joy.

(Matt. 8/21 - 22)

The dead bury the dead every day of the week. If you are a Priest, Pastor or Minister and you are not born again and in the Spirit, and the person you are burying is not born again and in the Spirit, then, you are the dead burying the dead ?

Then another of the disciples said to Him, "Lord, let me first go and bury my Father." But Jesus said to Him, "Follow Me, and let the dead bury their own dead". The man was putting things off by saying what he said. Jesus stresses the urgency to follow Him. We have no guarantee of to morrow, that is why I have no time for novenas that take ten days to complete, or rituals that do not bring a person to conversion on the spot.

Seeds need to be sown and watered.

So many people (creatures like you and I) die physically and spiritually because we lack the knowledge of the creator, who tells us how we should live in moderation, enjoy life to the full and bring up our children to know and love God.

If we lived as God says we should, followed His **COMMANDMENTS (commands meant)** to help us live longer, and be at peace with ourselves and others, we would have less child abuse, rape, domestic violence or divorce. Not need security locks on our doors, fewer people would die from sexually transmitted diseases, be murdered or commit suicide etc. and save the state a fortune on medical bills.

When the physical body packs in because of old age or sickness, abuse of the body, or dependency on substances like alcohol or drugs, the spirit body and soul of the person that is immortal never dies, ends up in hell, after it leaves the body unless the person has repented before they physically die. The earthly tent folds up, then the spirit body and soul is free to return to God for judgement or reward.

The bible, the creator's manual for His creatures, for me is a great way to present God's message to humanity.

My conscience was enlightened as to what was right and wrong.

The law and doctrine that I was brought up under, as I have already shared, could never have made me a Christian, but did enlighten my conscience as to what was right and wrong. I am grateful for the teaching given to me by my mam and dad and by my church. (Romans 7-7) "The law made me, know what sin was". (Romans 7-17) "As it is, it is no longer I myself who do it, but it is sin living in me". (Romans 7/18) "I know that nothing good lives in me, that is, in my sinful nature. For I have the desire to do what is good, but I cannot carry it out". (Romans 7/20) "Now if I do what I do not want to do, it is no longer I who do it, but it is sin living in me that does it". The apostle Paul was able to overcome, I was able to overcome. My nature changed to a Christ like nature, so can yours by the power of the Holy Spirit.

AS

I SHARE MY NOTES AND OBSERVATIONS, MY BEFORE AND AFTER EXPERIENCES OF THINGS TAUGHT ME, READ, HEARD SEEN AND REVEALED -THINGS DON'T ADD UP.

Some men and women both religious and lay, without portfolios, and false prophets to boot, still preach falsehoods and practice sectarianism.

The goal posts were moved and are moving all the time. The contradictions were and are too numerous to count.

As I compared what I was taught and brought up with as a young man, with Vatican II and the Bible, things did not add up.

Mary is the example from generation to generation as to how we should be obedient to God.

Man is only responsible for his own generation.

The institutional churches have ordained men and women whom God has not. They have created intercessors, mediators and advocates in the heavens and in the minds and hearts of men and women that cause confusion. They have no mandate or God given authority as teachers, and lead people astray, by not speaking spiritual truths and failing to tell them, that they must repent, be born again, and come into the knowledge of the Word of God.

Leaders of government, military and business are seldom judged by man on their personal lives. However Jesus will eventually judge them.

Teachers of the Word are subject to a special judgement by God.

Teachers of the Word are subject to a special judgement by the character they reveal, that is why and I say it again, I stick strictly to the Word of God. The following cannot be challenged often enough and I will say it a thousand times if I have to. That there are various groups within the Roman Catholic church, (other churches have their own problems) that have encouraged people from time immemorial to follow rituals, do holy things, do this, do that, say ejaculations, gain indulgences, do novenas, like novena of grace or say divine mercy prayers, light candles, abstain and fast, honour dead saints, pray in front of statues, have a shrine in their home, say rosaries, wear medals, without understanding that none of these things mentioned bring about conversion. Buses still continue to go here there and every-where to shrines, moving statues, and holy places.

STOP IT ALL

BE STILL AND KNOW

THAT JESUS CHRIST IS LORD.

These poor unfortunate people searching to fill that cavity of loneliness within them, believe in their ignorance what false prophets tell them. Some institutionally appointed men and women, people pleasers they do not even know, tell them what Mary has said at Knock, Medjugorje, Fatima, Lourdes, Guadalupe and the number of prayers needed to get you out of purgatory, instead of teaching the Word of God.

Ask yourself does purgatory exist. On second thoughts don't ask yourself, ask Jesus and tell him his death on the cross was not enough to save you, he should have done more.

We should encourage people to read the Word of God as Mary suggested, to see what Jesus says, instead they listen to Satan and his false prophets, what Mary is alleged to have said at various places around the world and believe them, instead of believing what God says.

WHY DO YOU BABBLE LIKE PAGANS ?

JESUS ASK'S THE CHRISTIANS.

(Matt. 6/7-6/32)

"And when you pray, do not keep on babbling like pagans, for they think they will be heard because of their many words. For the pagans run after all these things, and your heavenly Father knows that you need to eat and drink and clothe yourself".

I believe that every prayer I said, rosary or not was the prayer of a carnal Christian and I babbled like a pagan. I had not repented, and was not born again despite adhering to my religious duties, as a Roman Catholic.

I NOW KNOW THAT I AM A CHILD OF

GOD AND WHY...DO YOU?

Having accepted Jesus as my Lord and saviour, I have a right to be called a child of God (John 1/12-13) " but as many as received Him, to them He gave the right to become children of God, to those who believe in His name: who were born not of blood, nor of the will of the flesh, (like all humans) nor of the will of man, but of God". I must keep away from untruths, rituals etc. and running from one prayer meeting or holy shrine to another, being misled by unscriptured individuals who contaminate the word and are guided by a spirit of error rather than the Holy Spirit. Jesus charged his opponents with actual disobedience of God's commands through their slavish adherence to the oral law.

(Matt 15/8-9) "These people honour me with their lips, but their hearts are far from me. They (notice he did not say His people) worship me in vain; their teachings are but rules taught by men".

MY LIFE HAS CHANGED SINCE I CAME INTO THE KNOWLEDGE OF THE WORD OF GOD, SO CAN YOURS.

(Vatican II- Flannery, page 544 - 73)

I consider most of my activities of the past as empty rituals. Vatican documents say that ceremonies, however beautiful, or associations however flourishing, will be of little value if they are not directed toward educating men in the attainment of Christian maturity. We must move from being carnal Christians on milk, to solid food.

(Page 544, Flannery Vatican II, footnote 74)

St. Jerome asked "Of what use is it if the walls gleam with jewels and Christ dies in a poor man".

The futility of religious rituals, and the corruption of leadership was boldly spoken about in the following scriptures. Are things any different to day ?

(Amos 5/21-23) who was called to deliver God's message to the Northern Kingdom of Israel, written 760-750 BC. (approx. 2,750 years ago) "I hate and despise your feast days, and I do not savour your sacred assemblies, though you offer Me burnt offerings and your grain offerings, I will not accept them, nor will I regard your fattened peace offerings. Take away from me the noise of your songs, for I will not hear the melody of your stringed instruments". Is your church or the church I was born into guilty of the same things to day. If we do not repent and be born again our prayers become songs of lamentation and mourning.

I believe, if love and proper relationships are not maintained between me and God and me and my neighbour, I AM AN EMPTY PREACHER. (Mark 8/37-38) "Or what will a man give in exchange for his soul. FOR WHOEVER IS ASHAMED OF ME AND MY WORDS IN THIS ADULTEROUS AND SINFUL GENERATION, of him the son of Man also will be ashamed when he comes in the glory of His Father with the holy angels." written 65-70 AD. (1935 years ago). The old and New Testament readings, that I have quoted are just as relevant to day, two thousand years later.

The WORD will NEVER change and will be the same in the new heaven. Unscriptured individuals in the last two thousand years have defied this, and made God's out of Mary the mother of Jesus, Padre Pio, Faustina, St. Anthony and a host of others who may have been RECIPIENTS of God's graces, not distributors. (2 Tim. 3/16). "All scripture is given by inspiration of God, and is profitable for doctrine, for reproof, for correction, for instruction in righteousness". So why do we ignore the Word of God and allow so much holy rubbish to be taught.

I, measure all things against the scriptures. I am not in to Marian piety, Padre Pio piety, Faustina or any other cult.

I see signs and wonders everyday because I stick strictly to the written Word of God at all times. I pray the living word into all situations, by first bringing the person that has asked me to pray with them to repentance, seeking the kingdom first with the focus on conversion. Asking for and receiving the Holy Spirit, which is the first miracle, followed by conversion, faith, wisdom and discernment. You can cope when you pray within the will of the Father. The Word is the sword of the Spirit; the Holy Spirit is the third person of the Trinity. You cannot be a Christian if you do not believe this. If God is a spirit being and a person, so, is Jesus, so, is the Spirit, and so are we who are made in God's Spirit image and likeness, not physical, that is why we can never die. Our Spirit body is immortal and never dies.

(Genises 6/3)

Then the Lord said, "My Spirit will not contend with man forever, for he is mortal"

We live in a collapsible tent which is our physical body that will fold up within **one hundred and twenty years,** then the spirit body and soul returns to God to live forever in heaven or in hell with the devil and his angels. God sent his Word to heal us not any old Word or mans' pious opinion. Man can only do what is *humanly* possible to over come if he is not in the Spirit.

If man is in the Spirit, he finds he can ask God for *anything* in Jesus name. Miracles will happen for the reasons set out on the next page.

As a child of God I have the right to ask for a miracle.

When God's children pray after repentance, those born again and in the Spirit, they send God's living Word that He sent to heal us, back to Him. It never returns empty to those that are His and are born again. He watches over His Word. God CANNOT AND WON'T respond to words or pious opinions that are not His.

(1Cor. 4/6)

He will give us a heart to know Him, we are not to go beyond what is written. I believe only what is written, man is weak and limited. Blessed is he who reads the Word while the Holy Spirit imparts Spiritual truths.

The person of the Holy Spirit cannot move the sword , that is the Word, if God has not spoken it. I believe the church I was born into is a dead church full of pious opinions that has wandered and gone astray like most historical Christian churches because the spirit WAS and IS still missing. We need revival, the Spirit will move when we (Matt. 6-33) "Seek first the kingdom of God and His righteousness, and all these things shall be added to you". *We pray for His will to be done in everything. We pray for the coming of the kingdom. We pray for our daily necessities. We pray for forgiveness, and practice forgiven towards others. We pray for the leading of the Lord, and deliverance from evil. We are to pray in faith, for "without faith it is impossible to please Him". The model prayer is brief, to the point, and not repetitious. It is the perfect prayer the Lord's Prayer.*

THEY HAVE ITCHING EARS.

(2 Tim. 4//2-3)

I read in the word that you and I are to preach the word in season and out of season. Convince, rebuke, exhort with long suffering and teaching. For the time will come when they will not endure sound doctrine, but according to their own desires, because they have itching ears, they will heap up for themselves teachers: and they will turn their ears away from the truth, and be turned aside to fables. I believe this has happened to many people of the Roman Catholic tradition and others. We were denied knowledge of the Word of God. No Holy Spirit! No teaching! No conversion! No love!

(VATICAN II - IV. DEVOTION TO THE BLESSED VIRGIN IN
THE CHURCH PAGE 94 - FOOT NOTE 285)

**I have read Vatican II material on Mary the
mother of Jesus and her role, which it says
should be free of exaggeration
which I believe it is not in Ireland.** In the
Roman catholic church, it seems to me we have
churches within a church, and cults within cults.
(Divine Mercy, Padre Pio, Legion of Mary,
Latin rite groups, Matt Talbot groups, Marian
groups, Opus Dei groups, Immaculate Heart of
Mary groups etc.) I now wonder are we going to
bin all the things of Vatican II and what the
present Pope has talked about, for example. He
says "THE LAYMAN must be a witness as
modern man listens more willingly to witnesses
than to teachers, and if he listens to teachers it is
because they are witnesses." I am a witness and
it is my job and your job also, whether you are a
King, Queen, Pope or President to bring
something of to-morrow in to the world of today.

The present Pope also says "as Christians we
can justly consider, that the future of humanity
lies in the hands of those who are strong enough

to provide coming generations with a reason for living and hoping".

I believe for these things TO HAPPEN, our hope has to be in Jesus our first love, *NOT* Mary, Padre Pio, Faustina, St. Anthony, Blessed Martin, Matt Talbot or anyone else.

We replaced our God given Guardian Angel with St. Christopher, who has been dethroned in recent times. We must forget about this Roman Catholic, Protestant bit and get on with being Christian and worshipping God in Spirit and in truth. Where there is division and sectarianism there is no life in the Spirit. We have failed the present generation, so the future generations will suffer.

My body was not the temple of God's Holy Spirit, before my conversion.

I believe, as a young man I was praying litanies to powerless dead people that had no power. As deaf as they come, unable to hear me, as my mind wandered all around the world or I fell asleep during the rosary and missed half of the prayers to all the fifty saints that followed, before I went to my night classes.

We are still at it, there is no conversion in saying the rosary. The first half of the Hail Mary is biblical the second part is added by man of the flesh a pious opinion.

Down through the years countless countries, civilisations and churches like the church I was born into, the Roman Catholic Church and others, have ignored the call to evangelise, stand in the gap, take individual responsibility and help make a difference as the Pope has said. (2 Timothy 4/4-5) "It is written that they will turn their ears away from the truth, and be turned aside to myths. But you, (John Manning and all in Christ) keep your head be watchful in all situations, endure hardship, do the work of an evangelist, discharge all the duties of your ministry".

I believe that the message is singular to individuals and when they come together in Jesus name, they become the spiritual Church that God is building with Jesus as its foundation, silent and visible in action. God is not found in concrete or man made buildings or tabernacles that are visible, only where those in Christ (Human tabernacles) are gathered in his name then the ground becomes holy ground. Each generation is responsible for the church in it's own generation. Errors of teaching must be corrected. Too often we have comprised the truth, (Jeremiah 23/25-27) says, "Teachers know that the Lord will not hold anyone guiltless who speaks his own opinion in the Lord's name".

(Jeremiah 43/2-7) "Leaders DO NOT compromise the truth or alter God's word to appease men".

I am not afraid to speak up, I trust that the Lord protects those He sends to speak His word.

Ignorance of the law will not keep you out of prison if you break it .

I believe, that a lot of religious leaders, past and present, because they were party to sectarianism, and denominationalism have squandered the inheritance of our young people. Lack of knowledge of the law of the land will not keep you out of prison if you break the law. Lack of knowledge of the Word of God will not prevent you from going to hell and being accountable to God for what you teach when you die.

The Roman catholic church, the Protestant church, the Anglican church, the Lutheran church, the Methodist church, the Baptist church and all the old established denominational churches, some not mentioned, seem to me, were and still are, more concerned about spreading their doctrine by practicing sectarianism, than by building up the body of believers who are the church. The catechism of the catholic church (page 191 ref. 289-290) says this "The Church, then, is "the holy People of God", and her members are called " saints". I believe that all who are born again are living saints, followers of Jesus and are scattered within and outside of the denominational churches, which have high jacked the Word of God and contaminated it. They behave like politicians, where the party image is more important than the people the believers.

God is always in charge, building His spiritual church.
He is not into corporate denominations or sectarianism.

I was consistently taught to believe that I could earn God's love and acceptance by being good and doing good, observing certain rules and regulations, and by saying certain prayers, that became mantras, so I could stay in favor with God. Your spirit body cannot enter heaven when you die just because you are a member of a denomination. God does not give the Holy Spirit to a corporate body, group or church. He gives it to individuals who ask, living stones that make up the church, the body of believers. By the power of the Holy Spirit you can cope. We must be equipped like the apostles, who could not do a thing until they received power, neither can you or I.

THE GIFTS AND WHERE THEY COME FROM

Hebrews 2/4 is quite clear as to where the gifts come from

"GOD ALSO TESTIFIED TO IT BY SIGNS, WONDERS AND VARIOUS MIRACLES, AND GIFTS OF THE HOLY SPIRIT DISTRIBUTED ACCORDING TO HIS WILL"

1 Corinthians 12-11

"ALL THESE ARE THE WORK OF ONE AND THE SAME SPIRIT, AND HE GIVES THEM TO EACH ONE, JUST AS HE DETERMINES".

To believe that they come from Mary, I believe is a pious opinion and an untruth.

The Scripture on page 321 and the Scripture set out below contradict what is written in the book called

"THIS IS YOUR MOTHER"

God will prove you a liar if you teach what He has not said. Were not all the doomsday people of the past and present made liars of?

(Proverbs 30/5-6)

"Every Word of God is pure / flawless; He is a shield to those who take refuge in him. Do not add to His Words, or He will rebuke you and prove you a liar". I believe He will continue to do so until our lives become Christ centered like Mary's life was, by being obedient to God's Word. False teaching is carried on after the liar is dead. There are millions of people praying for years and their prayers are never heard or answered, they are worn out, sad, lonely and weary. When I pray with them on the help line or in person by the power of the Holy Spirit, I bring them to repentance and conversion in Christ and to the baptism in the Holy Spirit, where they find that peace that defies all human understanding. If I, when praying with people, *do not use* words given in the Scriptures, there will be no CONVERSIONS, NO HEALINGS and I, or whoever, will be made a liar. We must at all times pray within the will of the Father in Jesus' name.

If Mary Needed Salvation so does everyone else

You cannot put Mary on a level of equality with Jesus Christ as we have done in Ireland.

Mary, who is completely SUBORDINATE AND DEPENDENT ON HER REDEEMING SON, even for her own redemption, says, in that beautiful prayer the Magnificat, the song of Mary, (Luke 1/46) "My soul magnifies the Lord, And my spirit has rejoiced in God my SAVIOUR." If you believe different you are in error, you believe what man teaches and not what God teaches. *Flannery edition Vatican II page 86, says and I quote "At the same time, however, because SHE belongs to the offspring of Adam, she is one with all human beings in their need for salvation.*

Indeed she is clearly the mother of the members of Christ, since she co-operated out of love so that there might be born in the Church the faithful, who are members of Christ their Head".

HOW CAN VATICAN II, THE LEGION OF MARY AND OTHERS TEACH THINGS THAT ARE NOT OF THE WORD ?

WHY TEACH DOCTRINE THAT WE CANNOT SHARE WITH OTHER BELIEVERS ?

MARIAN PIETY HAS TAKEN OVER, SO HAS DEVOTION TO PADRE PIO, DEVINE MERCY ETC. AND JESUS, WHO GAVE HIS LIFE FOR US, IS SET ASIDE.

(1 Thess. 5/19)

IN ALLOWING THIS TO HAPPEN, WE HAVE STIFLED THE SPIRIT OR PUT OUT THE SPIRITS FIRE.

ALL TEACHING MUST BE IN AGREEMENT WITH THE GOSPEL, NO MATTER WHAT YOUR DENOMINATION.

Let God interrupt your life like he did Mary the mother of Jesus, Joseph her husband, Moses, Abraham, David and all of the prophets and apostles of the past, and present including myself as part of the born again people in various denominational, corporate and house churches. Jesus will take the believers, His people, out of the world when he comes back.

All Roman Catholics, Protestants etc. and those with tags will be left behind. If you snuff it out in the meanwhile before Jesus comes back and you have not repented or are not born again from above, you will go to hell, when you die. So it is written.

Mary said to God, THY will be done. Eve said MY will be done. Through the obedience of one woman, Mary the bearer of God's only son, God put his plan for redemption into operation. I believe Mary's role ended as she left the vicinity of the cross with John. The main line and new Christian churches are as bad as the political parties, where the party is more important than the people, and the denominations and doctrines more important than the people the believers.

It is written in the Word of God, where it says in

1 JOHN 5/4

"Everyone born of Him

overcomes"

> **THAT IS WHY I HAVE WRITTEN THIS BOOK ON COPING. IT IS FOR YOUNG AND OLD**

Jesus said trust in God and trust in me

GOD kept HIS promise to me and the people of the testimonies in this book and will to you. Seek His kingdom first and its righteousness.

It is worth repeating that we are born into the family of man. We must be re-born again into the family of GOD. Then, and only then, do we have the right to become children of GOD, and take on the nature of JESUS, no matter what denomination we belong to. God took me out of my religion for a few minutes, look what happened. Let him take you out of where ever you are and see what happens to you.

As an evangelist I share things received, things read, heard, seen and revealed, with references and confirmed by the Holy Spirit.

I must keep my vision beyond myself, keep my eye on the Lord, believe His Word that will never change and not be led astray by false prophets, who pass on rituals and false doctrines of the past that have failed miserably. You can pass on a doctrine, you cannot pass on FAITH, which is a GIFT to be asked for and received.

The driver of deceit ?

Those who practice and still teach rituals of the past, holy rubbish I call it, that causes division in the body and brings them into the new millennium, might find the message posted on the next page PINNED on the gate of heaven as they pass. The driver of deceit is changing the place of your destination on the front of the bus. You thought the bus was going to purgatory, then to heaven. I believe, as I have already said, purgatory does not exist-its hell or heaven. I am a coward.

NOTICE

(Matt. 7 /21-23)

"Not everyone who says to me, 'LORD, LORD, will enter the kingdom of heaven, but only he who does the will of my Father who is in heaven. "Many will say to me on that day, 'LORD, LORD,' did we not prophesy in your name, and in your name drive out demons and perform many miracles?' Then I will tell them plainly 'I never knew you. Away from me you evildoers!'

(Matt. 24/24)

"For false Christ's and false prophets will appear and perform great signs and miracles to deceive even the elect-if that were possible. See, I have told you ahead of time".

CHAPTER 4

The questions people ask.

Over the next number of pages I share with you, some of the questions people have asked me over the years and the answers I gave them on how to pray for specific needs. The things I said to them at meetings, on radio, here and in other countries, using the Scripture as a guide. Quotes from the text and true testimonies may be repeated in the question and answer section. You may not have the time to read the entire book or want to. However, there may be something to catch your eye in the question and answer section that might cause you to stop, think and question the things you believe or have been taught in your particular denomination and compare it with the Word of God that is timeless.

Does God allow divorce ?

(Matt. 5/32 - Good News Bible - Collins Catholic Edition)

I believe he does under certain circumstances. The Bible is for believers, the church, that God has taken out of the world, two or more, they are in the world but not of it. "It is written that everyone who divorces his wife, except for the case of fornication, (all sinful sexual activity/marital unfaithfulness, voluntary sexual intercourse of an unmarried person with someone of the opposite sex.) makes her an adulteress, and anyone who marries a divorced woman commits adultery". I personally believe that divorce is not the problem, but re-marriage is. God, the Father of the Trinity has given every person the gift of free will to believe and follow what ever God they wish to follow, and loves them whether they love him or not. If you repent to God in Jesus' name for all your sins, you will go to heaven when you die. It is your decision whether you should re-marry or not. If you are in the Spirit, the Holy Spirit will guide you as to what to do. I believe that only by the power of the Holy Spirit, can we find that peace that defies all human understanding and cope.

A decision prayer for those contemplating separation or divorce.

Heavenly Father, I come to you as a sinner. I have not robbed any banks nor have I murdered anyone, nevertheless I repent. I am sorry for all my sins from my head to my heart. In my brokenness, I ask you in Jesus' name to forgive me. I ask you now for the gift of the Holy Spirit, the gift of faith, wisdom and discernment and receive all. Heavenly Father, do not let me retain any sin of unforgiveness towards any person, help me forgive all who have hurt me, especially my husband/wife who wants to divorce or to separate. I know that if I retain any sin of unforgiveness towards any person, it is me that will suffer. Bring my husband/wife and myself closer to Jesus, who says "You cannot come to me unless my Father draws you". I thank you for the years with my husband/wife and my children. (if any) You have a plan for both of us, help me stand back and let you work it out in Jesus' name, Amen. I thank you for allowing this awful experience to happen to me and by the power of the Holy Spirit I will overcome.

John my mother asked at her age eighty two, where is Limbo ?

As I prayed with my mam who was not so well one Sunday morning, I felt a sadness in her and asked what was worrying her. She started to cry and asked me "where was limbo" and would she ever see her baby again who was still born and not baptized.   For the last nine months I have been thinking a lot about this, I cannot get it out of my mind. Are there windows in heaven, can you look out and see the babies in limbo? I was gob smacked, as I found out for the first time that my mam had a still birth some time after I was born. I was the eldest of ten. She had not spoken about this before and through the tears, I explained to mam that limbo was a lie and a terrible burden put on women, by sick church leaders, control freaks that did not know the Word of God and were not in the Spirit. I went to the Bishop's office and complained, asking how come this lie was never addressed and an apology given. I was told that it was a wrong teaching, and not taught anymore. Imagine the number of poor unfortunate mother's that believed what they were told and have gone to their graves sad and broken hearted believing such rubbish. The flesh body dies and the Spirit body returns to God to live forever, it is immortal, never dies. I told my mam that morning, four years before she died, that she would see her child fully developed as a spirit person like God is in heaven, as God had ordained with the eyes of her spirit body. We are made in Gods spirit image and likeness.

…Limbo was a lie

…is Purgatory a lie ?

read page 262 in chapter 2, then make your own decision.

John, would you please tell me what connection the devil has with the occult, a lot of it seems harmless.

The dictionary definition of the word occult is as follows:- Mysterious, supernatural, esoteric knowledge, hide from view, deceit or secret. Satan himself who is the ruler of this world controls the minds and hearts of men, women and children after they commit their first sin. (John 8/44) Tells us "That you belong to your father the devil, and you want to carry out your father's desire. He was a murderer from the beginning, not holding to the truth, for there is no truth in him". Satan's real name was Lucifer and was once a cherub in heaven, he lifted himself up in pride and rebelled against God who created him. He and one third of the angels were thrown out of heaven and came to live around the planet earth as spirit beings in opposition to God, to try and destroy what God, had created which includes man. Satan captures the hearts and minds of young and old when they do things in secret, like take drugs, drink to much, sniff glue, listen to the suggestive words of rock music.

Read Mary's story about the Ouija Board fun game on page 172/173.

God is not hearing my prayers ?

I read the following notice in a park and sea area, near beautiful San Clemente / Capistrano, California USA.

> **DO NOT FEED THE BIRDS OR ANIMALS, AS YOU CREATE DEPENDENCY. THE AREA ONLY FEEDS SO MANY.**

The Holy Spirit reminded me in the following scripture that God was their provider and I quote (Matt. 6/26) where Jesus says "Look at the birds of the air, for they neither sow nor reap nor gather into barns; yet your heavenly Father feeds them. Are you not of more value than they". I now know that I was brought up to depend on formulae, do novenas, wear medals and scapulars, partake in rituals and do all kinds of things that actually separated me from God and could not bring conversion - I almost starved to death on rituals! Read the healing and conversion prayer on the back page of this book, ask for the Holy Spirit and start praying all over again.

DOES HELL EXIST ?

How can you live in hell forever, if you are all burned up and nothing of you is left ?

This is what the Word of God says about hell...

(Luke 12/5)

Jesus tells the Disciples (you and I) not to fear their enemies, whose judgement is merely physical and temporal. They are to reverence God, whose judgement is final and of eternal consequences. He tells us whom we should fear; "Fear Him who, after He has killed, has power to cast into HELL; yes, I say to you, fear Him".

The tongue is so set among our members that it defiles the whole body, and sets on fire the course of our nature; and is set on fire by HELL.

(Luke 16/25) "The rich man died and in HELL where he was in torment, he looked up and saw Abraham far away, with Lazarus in his bosom. He called out to him", 'Father Abraham, have pity on me and send Lazarus to dip the tip of his finger in water and cool my tongue, because I am in agony in this fire'.

But Abraham replied, 'Son, remember that in your lifetime you received your good things, while Lazarus received bad things, now he is comforted here and you are in agony.' I believe, if we do not read, believe and listen to the Word of God, we will end up in hell.

So what do you think yourself ? The rich man could see with the eyes of his spirit body. Could hear, could feel, could talk, could understand, knew he was thirsty, there was water somewhere, he could think and reason, and had feelings for his family and knew then, when it was too late, that they should repent and believe in God. That was my first step, let it be yours.

Solomon was a very rich and fair man and despite his ups and downs, womanizing, counting his camels and his wives etc., he had a great relationship with God who loved him, whether he was good or bad. Whereas the rich man that ignored Lazarus, ignored God also.

It is no harm to be rich as long as Jesus is Lord of your life and your riches.

Some people never want to let go of their problems they become their God. When you have a good relationship with God and you are wealthy, then you can use your riches wisely. For some people money is their God.

You can never harm a spirit (ghost). It is our spirit body that goes to hell or heaven when the flesh body dies, to life everlasting or eternal damnation, it is our free choice. We are Spirit beings after all, God is a Spirit and a person. It is said that our skin renews itself every twenty eight days, and that if you and I were to sit under a big microscope we would not be able to see one another with all the debris floating around.

A PRAYER FOR THE FAMILY

MEMBERS

LEFT BEHIND AFTER A SUICIDE.

If you have had someone close to you who died by taking their own life, join me in the following prayer. I make my prayer a three-way conversation with myself, the person I am praying with to God in Jesus name, who won't join us if we do not repent. Nice words and prayers have no meaning, you might as well talk to the wall. Repentance makes prayer worthy, so I invite Jesus to be present. When you speak the Word, the Word becomes a living Word, if you are in the Spirit. The Spirit moves and the Word becomes the sword of the Spirit.

The prayer might go like this. "Heavenly Father I come to you as a sinner and I repent of all my sins, you know that my heart is broken. My son, (daughter, brother, wife or who ever) took his/own life and I feel very sad. I am burdened with guilt, I find it hard to cope, I lack understanding. My embarrassment causes me to shun people and friends. Could I have helped I ask myself ? As John and I search the depths of my emotions for understanding, I believe that there is a time and a place for everything, a time to die, a time to laugh, a time to cry. Nothing happens without you knowing it; you are the creator. John and I are creatures made in your spirit image and likeness. As we gather together in your name, seeking your kingdom first, help me believe in your Word and promises. Help me to forgive myself of all my failings and to forgive others who have hurt me. I have been hurt by the death of ? Do not let me retain any sin of guilt or blame in any shape or form, only you the creator and ? knew exactly what he /she was thinking at the time of their death. Only you know who is in heaven and who is not. You knew ? by their name, before you put him/her together in their mother's tummy. As I seek the kingdom and its righteousness, Jesus, I recall with John as we pray together, what you said in the Scriptures when someone wanted to know what was to happen to others. You said 'what is it to you, follow me'. I must do the same thing, follow you. Having repented, I ask you now for the gift of the Holy Spirit, the first of the gifts, then faith, wisdom and discernment.

Help me to believe that in Jesus' name, you my heavenly Father, will fulfill the plan you have for me, and give me the gift of discernment to apply to my every day activities and the decisions I have to make. I praise you and thank you, Jesus, as I rebuke all fears and anxieties in me that are not of you. I thank you for the years with ? make me the person you want me to be, not fearful or afraid.

Give me a desire for your Word, it is flawless, it is the lamp at my feet, let your Word dwell in me, fix your Word in my heart. I thank you for my awful experience, as it brought me closer to you my heavenly Father who draws me closer to Jesus my Lord and Savior. Amen".

Say a prayer with me I am sick.

When people who are sick phone or call for prayer, I always ask have they been to their doctor, and if not why not, well they say maybe God will heal me, so will you pray for a miracle.

I say, sure I will pray with you by seeking the kingdom first for you, then we will pray out the fear that you have of going to the doctor. When conversion takes place, the miracle can happen, having explained this I insist that they go to their doctor for a medical and they do. You could be seriously ill and not know it, go before it is too late, you could die in nine days waiting to finish the novena to saints canonized by man that may not be in heaven. You may find out that medication will help if the ailment is caught in time. If the medical is clear and you do not feel well, or if the doctor says you have a problem, either way come back for a prayer and a chat.

John, talk to me about 'out of body' experiences.

It is said that we only use between 1 and 10% of our physical eyesight, brain and other senses in this world, no one person really knows. I have prayed with quite a few people who have had and survived this type of 'out of body' experience. I could talk for hours on the subject. I am sure you have seen and heard people share their stories on television. I believe every human person born, has a spirit body that is immortal, and a physical body that is mortal, we are living souls. The spirit body is immortal, and indwells our physical body, you cannot hurt or kill it, and it has a covering of skin that makes me visible. Our resurrection body is our spirit body a living soul. Our human body, is a terrestrial body of the earth, living on land, it can be killed or injured. It is written in Psalm one hundred and thirty nine, "for You formed my inward parts; You covered me in my mother's womb", (did He cover my Spirit body) ? Had God not, you would not see me, I am a spirit being, made in God's Spirit image and likeness. I am like a tent, a tabernacle, an earthen vessel, a temple. My physical body will fall away some day and turn to dust, and be no more. My spirit body will never die, but will live forever in heaven or in hell. Invite Jesus into your life now. Some of my friends who have had this 'out' of body experience shared with me what they saw. Some saw a hand, some saw lights, some saw people that were recognisable. Some were looking down on themselves after accidents, looking down on themselves in the operating theatre, and could name the nurses and doctors whom they knew and their order of entry to the operating theatre, all kinds of happenings. I believe they could hear and see with the eyes and ears of their spirit bodies. We are spirit beings, made in God's Spirit image and likeness, which is not of flesh and blood.

How come God causes so much sickness ?

God does not cause sickness, he allows us to be sick or have accidents, by natural law. He also said in the beginning when he spoke creation into existence. (Genesis 1/29)"I have given you every herb that yields seed which is on the face of all the earth, and every tree whose fruit yields seed; to you it shall be for food". A lot of sickness in the world today is caused by man himself, by the way he lives, the abuse of his body, particularly in the area of sexually transmitted diseases, abuse of substances and the atmosphere, that harm his body and cause sickness. In my sickness, my wife's sickness, and in our brokeness and loneliness, finding it hard to cope, we turned to God the Father of the Trinity. Something good came out of our experiences and it will for you as it did for the people of the stories in this book.

God sent His Word to heal us, we are healed in Jesus' name, if we could believe it.

My self-esteem is in my boots, what prayer would you suggest ?

(John 6/44)

None, just say the following prayer from your head to your heart. Heavenly Father, I come to you, with my self esteem in my boots, please help me. I accept your son Jesus as my Lord and Saviour. I repent for all my sins, and forgive all who have ever hurt me. I ask for the gift of the Holy Spirit and I receive it in Jesus' name as I rebuke the spirit of low self-esteem that prevents me from being at peace with myself and others. You love me as I am, help me love myself, then I can love others. Thank you Jesus. Heavenly Father, I ask in Jesus' name that you bring me closer to your son Jesus who says "That no- one can come to me unless the Father draws him, and I will raise him up on the last day" Make me the person that you want me to be and help me walk tall. Only God the Father of the Trinity has the power to do this no one else. Mary the mother of Jesus, the apostles while they were alive could help. Padre Pio, St. Anthony etc. and others that man has canonized have no power, so no help.

Why do some laymen, priests and clergymen turn to prostitutes?

There are lots of reasons. I believe that if you have taken the vow of chastity (no genital sex if you are not married) that you do not have to take, as all human beings, clergy and lay, men and women, are expected by God to keep His commandments. But if you are not in the Spirit it is almost impossible to keep this vow, you deny yourself the joy of sex. Those who cannot cope go to prostitutes, or are in relationships with a male or female, and change partners on a regular basis, turn to masturbation, obesity, or to the abuse of substances, drink or drugs. Some men can survive without being married and practice celibacy. However the lack of genital sex is a different kettle of fish. After all, God put the plumbing together and it works. It is very difficult to deny the desires of the flesh, however, it can be done by the power of the Holy Spirit.

My wife won't have sex with me anymore since she had her last baby. I am tempted to have sex on the side.

Set out below is what God says about fulfilling marital duty and may help you avoid the temptation of having sex on the side. I suggest you say the healing and conversion prayer at the back of the book. Rebuke the spirit of desire.

(1 Cor. 7/3/4/5)

A man should fulfill his duty as a husband, and a woman fulfill her duty as a wife, and each should satisfy the other's needs. A wife is not the master of her own body, but her husband is; in the same way a husband is not the master of his own body but his wife is. Do not deny yourselves to each other, unless you first agree to do so for a while in order to spend time in prayer; but then resume normal marital relations.

I believe that Married couples should have normal sexual relations. Permanent abstinence deprives the other partner of his or her natural right and may lead to one or the other going else where. Lots of women in Ireland do not think that they have to have sex with their husbands after they have had their babies. Some men have told me that it drives them crazy; they then masturbate and often go to prostitutes, while others are tempted but do not. Both husband and wife have conjugal rights and exclusive possession of the other in this area, and should not deprive each other. *If you are the guilty one, I believe you break your marital vows.*

Say a prayer with me to help me give up gambling.

Say the healing and conversion prayer on the next page.

Everything we have, every breath we take, comes from God, He is the creator and we are His creatures. God is in control of all things. The money we make comes from God, He is our provider. He does not like us to gamble away His provision on the turn of a roulette wheel or card. Gambling can destroy a person, becoming an obsession and a compulsion just like alcoholism. The habitual gambler ruins his family and his life, and some have stolen to get money for gambling. It is like a disease. Gambling in any form, including the lottery, teaches people that fame, success, and fortune are available without work or struggle and undermines the virtues of commerce, manufacturing, investment and patience, which we replace with greed, lust, sloth (lazy, idle) or live for the moment mentality.

Talk to God in Jesus' name in the following prayer and ask him to help you give up gambling.

Heavenly Father, I come to you in my brokenness; it is written that I must seek your kingdom first.

I know I cannot hide anything from you. You know I gamble, which causes me to cheat on people who trust me and rely on me, including my wife, children, friends and employers. I cannot keep up this pretence any longer. I am sorry for all my sins and I ask you, my Heavenly Father, to help me in Jesus' name, as I repent.

Why do I do it Lord ? Only you know the nature of my personality. Is it because I want to be rich, I do not know ? Only you can fill the loneliness I feel. As John and I pray together I confess I am a sinner and repent. Help me not retain any sin of unforgiveness towards anyone. It is written that if we seek the kingdom first everything else will be given unto us. I need everything, Lord, now in whatever order you wish, as I ask you for the gift of the Holy Spirit, and receive him, the comforter, that is greater than the spirit within me who causes me to gamble. I rebuke any spirit within me that is not of you. My body, which you call a house, temple, tabernacle or earthen vessel has a wrong tenant at the moment that causes me to gamble. Bind the spirits in me that are not of you. Still my thoughts and mind and set me free in Jesus' name. Now that I have received the Holy Spirit, I ask for the gifts of faith, wisdom and discernment in Jesus' name and accept them. I praise and glorify your holy name, help me stand back and let you fulfill the plan you have for me. The next time I am tempted, John says, as the thought comes I am to reject it in Jesus' name and tell Satan to get lost as I have a future and he has none.

I broke my confirmation pledge, because of this, I have not gone to church for years, I feel God does not love me because I broke my promise.

When you come to know the Word and read it you will find that God's love is unconditional and that there is nothing that you have ever done, no promise you have ever broken, that prevents God from loving you, just as you are. People need to be converted, to be born again of the Spirit of God from above first, then you can do all things in moderation. So say the healing prayer on the last page of this book, tell God that you repent for all your sins. We should not be asking people to take pledges, or make promises they cannot keep in their own strength. The guilt is awful when they fail. People do not need pioneer pins, they need Jesus in their lives, then they can over come their problems and enjoy a drink in moderation.

A medium, told me I would die young.

PRAY THE HEALING PRAYER AND READ THE FOLLOWING SCRIPTURES.
READ WHAT GOD SAY'S ABOUT MEDIUMS., (Deut. 18/10-11-12
Lev. 20/6-27 - 1Sam. 28/7 - Iss. 29/4 - 8/19 Matt. 24/24)

God has a plan for us all and only He knows when He is going to call you home. Fortune telling, tarot cards, witchcraft, mediums etc. are all of the new age and are satanic and demonic. It amazes me the amount of prime time slots these people, who promote the occult get on T.V and radio. God says:- "When men tell you to consult mediums and spiritualists, who whisper and mutter, should not a people inquire of their God? Why consult the dead on behalf of the living? To the law and to the testimony! If they do not speak according to his Word, they have no light of dawn". Reject spiritual counsel from anyone who does not speak according to the Word of God. Avoid any form of the occult or spiritualism. "For false Christ's and false prophets, will appear and perform great signs and miracles to deceive even the elect-if that were possible. See, I have told you ahead of time".

(Satan can produce miracles in any name, but not in Jesus' name).

Read page 328 in this book - It is not God's voice mediums hear).

Mam and Dad are separating, could you pray with me that they won't.

God knows how you feel. He knows how your mam and dad feel towards one another also. There is nothing that you can hide from him. For prayer to be answered you must repent and at all times pray within the will of the father, in Jesus' name. If mam and dad do not love one another anymore there is nothing you can do, however nothing is impossible for God. When you are born again from above you have a right to be called a child of God (John 1/12-13) you become a living saint and when you pray, the Spirit of Christ within you moans and groans to God the Father for the things he knows you want before you ask.. Don't blame yourself or your brothers or sisters, because man and dad are separating. You cannot force one person to love another when love grows cold. Add the following to the healing prayer on page 429 ... I thank you heavenly Father for my mam and dad and their years together, help me stand back and allow you to fulfill the plan you have for them and us as a family and as individuals. I rebuke any spirit that keeps them apart in Jesus' name.

I have a fear of exams, what saint should I pray to ?

None. We do this all the time in Ireland, praying to saints who have no power, and may not even be in heaven. Read the sinner/conversion prayer on the last page of this book and ask God yourself, rebuke that spirit of confusion and fear within you, in Jesus' name just before you go into the exam room. Ask the Holy Spirit to go ahead of you, help and calm you, and God to fulfil the plan he has for you. Fear does not come from God. However, before the exams ever start, you should pray and study, and have a vision for the future by seeking God's kingdom first. He has a plan for you, stand back and let him work it out. Ask God in Jesus' name to help you with your studies. If you do not study why should you get help. So, who or what prevents you from studying? Is it laziness, low self esteem or fear? whatever it is, pray it out, by saying the healing and conversion prayer at the back of the book. Why should we seek the dead on behalf of the living. Read page 354 in the question and answer section of this book.

I lost my virginity, I feel so sad.

You broke God's law ; You would also feel sad if you robbed a bank and got caught or picked up a sexually transmitted disease. You could have become pregnant also. However, all you have to do is repent. When you repent remember what Jesus said to the woman caught in adultery, "go and sin no more". He says the same to you. God knows you are sad he wants you to be happy. He has already forgiven you for committing that sin of fornication, so forgive yourself, and the other person like God has forgiven you. Tell God you repent in Jesus' name, and ask for the gift of the Holy Spirit receive it and ask Him to fulfil his plan for you in Jesus' name. God still loves you whether you have repented or not.

There is always guilt after sex outside of marriage, no matter who you are. So Jesus says, "go and sin no more".

John, do you think things are better in this generation than they were in the past ?

From the comfort zone point of view, yes I do. The sinful nature of men and women has never changed since the fall of our first parents. God has given man the ability to be creative as creatures, however, He is the creator of all. Men and women were created for marriage, a state created by God for procreation. Modern technology and life styles have prevented this from happening. Young people cannot afford to have babies, as it costs a fortune to pay mortgages and baby minders. They cannot afford to be out of work, both parents have to work because we live in a two-pay cheque economy and work extraordinary hours, in trying to keep up with the changes in technology, and delivering babies to/from babysitters. If you want to call that living, that's fine. When Dolores and I got married, we could live on what I earned, paying bills with nothing to spare. Things are no different today except that we are more materialistic. We live and always have lived in a world of mismanaged minds.

Abortion or divorce should not be allowed, what do you think John ?

I recently received in the post a three colour brochure which said, that a nation that murders it's own children is a nation without a future. The world without Christ has no future don't mind the nation. Unless we are evangelized in this country and get away from the history of holy rituals and bring people in to the knowledge of the Word of God, we as a nation are lost. A religious nation gone astray, so are your children and mine. Jesus said in Luke 23/28 "Don't cry for me, but for yourselves and your children". God's Word is timeless and what He said to the women of Jerusalem two thousand years ago had many meanings which I believe apply to-day. We have broken hearts, broken homes, Abortion and all kinds of perversion. Christ left this command to us: "Therefore beseech the Lord of the harvest to send out workers into the harvest" We need Spirit filled people to preach the Word of God. God cannot bestow blessings or peace in a persons heart, prevent abortion or divorce unless the Holy Spirit moves and touches them. God loves you no matter what your sin.

I am a sex pervert.

I would not ask my wife to do the things I like to do with other women when away from home. My wife thinks I am just great, I need a chat. I am living a terrible lie.

Over a couple of weeks of chatting etc. we eventually got down to saying the sinners prayer, where he rebuked the sexual desires of the flesh in Jesus' name. The guilt that comes with this kind of carry-on is fierce, it can really screw up your marriage and your life. It is not like what God intended the marriage state to be. The nature has to change from the Adam and Eve nature, to our new nature in Christ. By the power of the Holy Spirit you will over come. My friend can now see a change in his life, it is not easy, however he is getting there.

I am dry and off the drink, but cannot find peace.

Say the sinner/conversion prayer on the next page.

(John 1/12-13)

Jesus gives us the gift of peace that defies all understanding, it is long term, permanent and free. However, it is not available to you if you are not born again. "Yet to all who received him, to those who believed in his name, he gave the right to become children of God - children born not of natural descent, nor of human decision or a husband's will, but born of God".

The way you feel is quite common and there are millions like you in Ireland and all over the world, who can stay off the drink and have no peace. There are many who stay off the drink and are just as crooked, dishonest and as obnoxious (disliked), molest their wives and children in different ways, cheat on them, leave them, divorce them, commit adultery etc., and think because they do not drink anymore they are just great. However, there are those who are great but they are few and far between.

Their nature has not changed. By the power of the Holy Spirit the nature can change to a Christ-like nature if you have that desire. Nothing is impossible for God.

The following is a healing prayer I say with people who are off the drink but have no peace.

Heavenly Father, in my brokenness I come to you, I am fed up and browned off. I drank all my own money and the money I married into. I am still paying loans back, well trying to but not too successfully. My wife has gone into another relationship and ignores me, I cannot visit, and my children do not want to know me, nor can I afford a divorce. I am as low as anyone can be. Heavenly Father, I repent for all my sins from my head to my heart. I ask you to help me love myself and forgive myself like you forgive me and love me. I am sorry for all the trouble that I have caused due to my drinking. I am sorry for not supporting my wife and children as promised in my marital vows. Help me understand where it says in your Word, "Whose sins you shall forgive they are forgiven and whose sins you shall retain they are retained".

Help me to understand that I must accept responsibility for my self and my actions and not retain any sin of unforgiveness towards any person living or dead, if I do, it is me that will suffer. I repent in Jesus' name for all my sins and accept Jesus your only son as my Lord and Saviour. I seek your kingdom first as John and I gather to pray and ask for the gift of faith first, and then the gift of the Holy Spirit, wisdom and discernment, I accept all in Jesus' name. I now rebuke in Jesus' name the spirit of loneliness, despair, low self esteem, fear, guilt and any spirit that comes at me that is not of you. Heavenly Father in Jesus' name make me the person you want me to be.

I cannot sleep at night.

Say the healing and conversion prayer on page 429 of this book. When you lie down to go asleep, say Jesus I am going to sleep in your name. I thank you for the gift of the Holy Spirit that never sleeps and allows my mind rest. I rebuke any spirit not of you that keeps me from sleeping, in Jesus' name.

***John, the following questions were asked at our
prayer group.***

*Please explain the "Immaculate Conception", we
have varied opinions at our prayer group.*

Some people teach that the immaculate
conception refers to the immaculate conception
of Mary which states that she was born without
sin. As I have already explained in the text, in
my quote from page 86, Flannery edition of
Vatican II and I quote it here again. "At the
same time, however, because she belongs to the
offspring of Adam she is one with all human
beings in their need for salvation".

Were Mary and Joseph married

or shacking up?

Because of things read, seen and heard, I believe
that when Mary was between thirteen and
fourteen years old her father, (as was the custom,
in first century Israel during the time of the
Roman Empire) arranged that Mary, his
daughter, would marry a chap by the name of
Joseph, a carpenter. Her role in life was now
set.

She was born into a Jewish family; her role in history would speak for itself.

The Angel Gabriel who appeared to Mary explained that she was chosen by God, to be the mother of His only son Jesus. " How will this be", Mary asked the Angel "since I am a virgin." (one who has not had sexual intercourse) It is obvious that Mary knew the facts of life, just like young girls do today, 2,000 years later. The Angel answered "That the Holy Spirit will come upon you and the power of the most high will overshadow you. So the Holy one to be born will be called the Son of God".

"I am the Lord's servant", Mary answered, "may it be done to me as you have said." Then the Angel left her. Mary knew that she was in big trouble now, facing shame and humiliation. Attitudes have not changed very much. Mary in faith, willingly submitted to God's will. Mary thought that Joseph might not marry her now, as he might consider her "damaged goods", no different today. However she acted with great courage and faith in God. When you became engaged in those days, (in Mary's time pledged to be married) sexual relationships were not allowed by Jewish law. The engagement could only be broken by divorce. This had Joseph worried also, as he did not want to expose Mary to public disgrace. Mary could have been stoned.

You can see that Joseph had a few things to worry about also. God told Joseph in a dream that he would marry Mary despite her pregnancy. (Matthew 1- 24-25) So when Joseph woke up, he did marry Mary, as the angel of the Lord had told him to do but had no sexual relations with her before she gave birth to her son. At the cross, Jesus saw His mother in shock because of what she was witnessing. He let her and John know, just like he tells us, the believers today, that they would be cared for after His death and resurrection. This respect God had for Mary applies to all women, an attitude not expected in the culture of that time and which still prevails today. Jesus, - God in the flesh - unlike men in His time and culture, thought that women were equal to men in the sight of God and could receive God's forgiveness and grace. The women were the first witnesses to His resurrection.

When my mam became pregnant with me, it was because the veil of my mother's hymen was broken from the outside, my father penetrated or entered my mam in the way God ordained. If my mam and dad had not been married, I would be born out of the sin of fornication, sex before marriage. It is not a sin to have sex or get pregnant if you are married, you do not break God's law. In Mary's case the veil of the hymen was broken as Jesus came down the birth canal into life, no penetration by man.

What does the word Incarnation mean ?

I have already said that Jesus had to be born of a human sinful mother, specially chosen by God, if Jesus was to be truly man, God in the flesh.

(I quote from the Catechism of the Catholic Church page 103 - *461*)

Taking up St. John's expression, "The Word became flesh", the Church calls it "Incarnation" the fact that the Son of God assumed a human nature in order to accomplish our salvation in it. In a hymn cited by St. Paul, it goes on to say that the Church sings the mystery of the Incarnation.

Having this in mind yourselves, which is yours in Christ Jesus, who, though He was in the form of God, did not count equality with God a thing to be grasped, but emptied himself, taking the form of a servant, being born in the likeness of men. And being found in human form he humbled himself and became obedient unto death, even on a cross. Hebrews 10/5-7 confirms.

John which church is the right church ?

Some bulbs in the chandelier are lighting and some bulbs are not.

I see all of the institutional churches that man controls as bulbs in a chandelier. Since the real church came into being two thousand years ago at Pentecost, we have in each generation since, some bulbs in the chandelier that are lighting and some bulbs that are not, meaning the living and the dead. *We have Roman Catholic/catholics. Protestant/catholics. Anglican/catholics. Presby -terian/catholics. Methodist/catholics. Baptist/ catholics etc.* All born again people are catholic, Spirit filled Christian believers. They are the real church of the Creed with Jesus as head. They are the bulbs that are lighting in the denominational sectarian chandelier.

"A man at a prayer meeting told me, that if I did not go to a Roman Catholic Priest for confession, my sins would not be forgiven".

He certainly won't go to heaven when he dies if he continues to teach such rubbish!

Through the tears she explained that all her family are protestant, she married into the Roman Catholic church, her mam was dead and never went to a priest for confession, is she in hell ? "Will the rest of my family go to hell if they die without going to a Roman Catholic Priest for confession"? Your sins are already forgiven in Jesus' name if you have repented. By His death and resurrection we are saved from the consequences of sin, repent to God the Father in Jesus name and be set free. By his death on the cross he has redeemed the world, but those not born again in the Spirit, have not come into that knowledge. They are still in darkness like the man who spoke with you. All who repent and die in Christ that are born again go to heaven, so it is written. Say the healing prayer at the back of the book. There are no denominations in heaven only born again Christians, who may be in a denomination.

So many people, clergy and lay, take on the role of teaching in the Roman Catholic Church who have not kept up to-date with the changes in Vatican II, lead people astray because they lack the knowledge of the word of God. No priest or pastor can forgive sin or retain sin; they can only remind us that our sins are forgiven in Jesus name. Pray for that man that hurt you so much, forgive him, he is preaching pure rubbish. You focus on the Lord, be born again and you and your household will be saved. Remember that there are no Protestants, Baptists, Roman Catholics or any other man-made group in heaven. Being a member of a club will not get you into heaven, only those born again of the Spirit from above will go to heaven when they die. So it is written in the Word.

John what about Fr. Anthony de Mello SJ. and his writings. I have read many of his teachings, and some trouble me.

I have read some of his writings and I have also heard some priests within the Roman Catholic church preach and quote him. I certainly cannot go along with a lot of what he teaches. I just read the Word of God that is timeless and rely on the Holy Spirit to give me understanding.

If you require any more information about Fr. Anthony de Mello SJ* :- Write to the Congregation for the Doctrine of the faith, c/o Veritas, asking for a copy of the notification concerning his teachings like I did. They say that some of his teachings are not compatible with the Roman Catholic faith and can cause grave harm. I agree with them.

* Veritas, Abbey Street, Dublin, Ireland should have a copy of the notification, as to why Fr. Anthony de Mello SJ. was dumped. However I also believe that the church that I was born into have a lot of questions to answer in relation to wrong teaching and I have mentioned a few in this book.

Thom asked why church goers seem so sad?

There are lots of people in the world today that are sad. It has nothing to do with going to church or mass. It has to do with having the Spirit of Christ live in you. * The Apostle Paul says "In fact unless you possessed the Spirit of Christ you do not belong to Him - the Spirit of God must live in you ! If not you live in darkness". How can you be happy, if you live in darkness. Rituals do not cause conversion or bring joy to your heart. **Jesus rebuked the undermining of Scriptures through man-made tradition when he said; "The worship they offer me is worthless, the doctrines they teach are only human regulations. You put aside the commandments of God to cling to human traditions. In this way you make God's Word null and void for the sake of your traditions which you have handed down". ***Now then, why do you try to test God by putting on the backs of the disciples a yoke that neither we or our fathers have been able to bear". I was fed on rituals and taught to believe pious opinions that became yokes. The church I was born into forgot its first love. If the Spirit of Christ does not live in you, you live in darkness.

* Romans 8 ** Mark 7/7-13 *** Acts. 15/10 explain the reasons

Why did God cause a famine in Ireland ?

In 1999 I was in discussion with a group of people in the USA, when a person started to talk about the famine in Ireland. This learned man stood up and was going on and on about the famine. I got fed up and interrupted him and asked him where he got his information from and told him that he was misinformed. "Well" he said "it is all recorded in this book that I am reading".

The silence was massive ?

I explained in the following way to the group of stunned people. We did not have a famine in Ireland, for a famine is where you have nothing. There was a potato blight sure, no potatoes the staple diet of the people was gone. but there was cabbage, lettuce, beet root, carrots, scallions, wheat, barley, corn and lots of other foods available. That were shipped along the highways to various ports of Ireland under armed guard, and then to England, as mammies, daddies and children died from hunger in pits, only yards away from the same highways. *It believe it was ethnic cleansing, not a famine.* We should never forget or allow it to happen again.

My children are shacking up with partners and do not go to mass. I am afraid that if they die, they will go to hell, I am very worried.

(1 Tim.2 - 1/2)

Going to mass or Holy Communion will not get you into heaven if you die. Marriage is God's plan for populating heaven. God has created the order of community - that is marriage, family, economic activity, Government and state. Satan, unable to create anything himself, tempts others to distort and misuse what God has created. God loves you whether you love Him or not, shacking up or not, living and having babies out of the sin of fornication or not. However, we all suffer the consequences of our actions and will be judged accordingly. If we die without repentance and being born again, our spirit body that never dies will go to hell. Say the healing and conversion prayer in this book, pray yourself, your partner and your children into the Kingdom of God who does not bless situations that he has not ordained.

John Manning, do you visit graveyards ?

No, I do not. Soon after my dad died my mam asked me "was I at the grave since his burial? I said "no mam", she said "You are right, sure he is not there". If I was in the area I would drop by to check on things. The memory of mam and dad are in my heart and my prayer at the grave would be, thank you Lord for using my mam and dad as instruments for procreation to give life to me. I will meet their spirit bodies in heaven.

I had an abortion, does God still love me or am I a murderer?

I believe, when you have an abortion, you abort the plan, God the creator had for the baby in your tummy to experience this temporary world.

You killed the flesh that covered the spirit body and soul of the child that God intended to grow to adulthood in this world. Our flesh makes us visible. You committed a FORGIVEABLE SIN; that does not prevent God from loving you just as you are. The spirit body of the child has returned to God, to be fulfilled as God had intended.

When you repent to God for all your sins including the abortion, they are forgiven in JESUS name, and Jesus would say to-you go and sin no more, like he said to the woman caught in adultery.

I have spoken on the telephone and prayed with lots of women who have had abortions. A high percentage I have never met, which does not matter, they ring for prayer and a chat, I tell them about God's unconditional love. The mammy always loses out, the daddy may have done a runner, the mam cannot cope and is misguided by people who try to normalise their own activities, because maybe they have had an abortion or whatever and others follow. People say sure everyone is doing it, they are not. The flash backs, the guilt and fear, the low self esteem and sleepless nights, are hard to cope with after you have had an abortion, so some women have told me when I pray with them. I believe them. This cancer scare that they believe is related to abortion, I believe is caused by guilt. However my job is to tell you that Jesus can set you free from bondage, guilt etc. If your are sick your health will improve as your emotions heal.

I say the prayer on the next page, 378 with anyone who has had an abortion.

All the prayers I make up are from scripture. Having brought the person to repentance that makes prayer worthy, I send God's Word back to Him when I pray and it becomes the sword of the Spirit, He watches over it, and it never returns empty. He sent His Word to heal us emotionally and physically. *The Prayer is based on Psalm 139. Read it if you wish or give it to someone.*

"Heavenly Father, you put me together in my mother's womb. You knew me by my name before my mam and dad. You also knew the baby that I aborted by name. John and I are gathered together in Jesus' name, on this telephone. I repent for all my sins including the taking of the life of my baby. I have missed out. Heavenly Father, you have not. I believe as I share and follow John in prayer, that I can come to a conversion experience in Christ, like John did. I aborted the plan you had for the baby in my tummy for this world. I have not aborted the plan you had for the spirit body and soul of my baby in the next world, where he/she will live forever in fullness, just like you had ordained. I ask you heavenly Father to help me to forgive the babies' dad, forgive myself and love myself. I ask you for the gifts of the Holy Spirit, the first of the gifts and receive it in Jesus' name. I ask for the gift of faith, wisdom, discernment and receive them just as I would a gift. I thank you for allowing me populate heaven with a Spirit person like you are. I praise and glorify you and ask that you fulfil your plan for me in Jesus' name. I thank you for allowing me help to populate heaven with a Spirit person like you are. I   thank you for what I have been through emotionally etc. This awful trauma brought me closer to Jesus, who says that you cannot come to him unless the Father draws you. God you see into our hearts, and know what the thought of the Holy Spirit is, as the Spirit pleads with God on behalf of his people and in accordance with his will. I thank you Jesus Amen. Help me go now and sin no more".

John, what do you think about novenas.

I am not into novenas. How do you know you will be alive in nine days?

I believe tomorrow is a period nowhere to be found, except perhaps, in the fool's calendar when the idle man works, the thief becomes honest, the drunkard sober. "Behold, now is the acceptable time" the day of salvation. Repent and invite Jesus to come live in you right now, you have no guarantee of tomorrow. I introduce people to Jesus by the power of the Holy Spirit, I move on, they remember Him not me.

God's call is not a call for tomorrow but for today. The women at the well needed Christ before she needed a church, a Redeemer before she needed a ritual. Jesus said. " I who speak to you am He". I want others to know Jesus like I do and the people of the stories in this book do.

The satisfaction in a man or woman's soul is completed in a living knowledge of Jesus Christ.

Is Holy Communion the bread of life ?

Is Jesus really in the tabernacle ?

If he really was present you would have a queue from the tabernacle in your local church to China and back.

I believe that the Word Jesus is the bread of life. I receive Holy Communion because Jesus says I should, in memory of Him. It is a mystery that I do not understand nor should I try. I believe that the bread should be called the bread of the presence.

(John 1/14)

"And the Word became flesh and dwelt among us, and we beheld His glory, the glory as of the only begotten of the Father full of grace and truth". Jesus identified Himself with humanity by becoming flesh and being born of an ordinary woman who was a sinner. God's Word is timeless and because it is, what happened at the last supper should happen as often as possible when the believers, those born again get together to celebrate in memory of Him.

Why do we not have Holy Communion under both species ?

(JOHN 1/1)

In the beginning was the Word and the Word, was with God. The Word is Jesus Christ, the eternal, ultimate expression of God.

Until the twelfth century, it was the common and accepted practice for the faithful in most dioceses to receive Communion under the two species of bread and wine.

From the thirteenth century to Vatican II the practice was discontinued, and restricted to the celebrant. After Vatican II, the Roman Catholic Church reverted to the custom of the early church, and the faithful are now able to receive Communion under both species. (Roman Catholic Encyclopedia, page 290). Why we do not, I do not know, maybe the numbers are great, ask your parish priest. I believe we should receive under both. Prior to 1215 people received Holy Communion less and less frequently. In 1215 the fourth Lateran Council felt obliged to prescribe annual communion at Easter time.

I believe that we cannot separate Holy Communion and the Word. I also believe the Word made flesh is Jesus who is the Bread of Life that feeds our Spirit Body and soul. Communion for me is a mystery that I cannot understand. I take Holy Communion in obedience because Jesus says I should in remembrance of Him. His Word is timeless and is relevant today and to morrow.

Is there life out there beyond the earth ?

There sure is. Jesus is coming back, he will visit the earth again but only God the Father knows when.

Paul says he was caught up in the third heaven, he does not know whether he was in the body or apart from the body, God knows. If there is a third heaven it is reasonable, I believe, to expect a second heaven.

(2Cor. 12/2)

Paul was caught up in paradise and heard inexpressible words, which he was not to repeat. Did not Jesus say to the thief on the cross, (Luke 23/43) "Assuredly, I say to you, today (not 10 years from now) you will be with Me in paradise" I believe the present heaven, is the holding place for all who have died in Christ waiting to come back with Jesus. I believe that people who have 'out of body' experiences like Paul's experience, see things with the eyes of their spirit bodies.

Enoch and Elijah went direct to God without having to die. We will never find the third heaven by using existing radio telescopes, jets or rocket ships. The names of those who have seen and written descriptions of extraterrestrial life are Isaiah, Jeremiah, Ezekiel, Paul and John. Their accounts are found in the old and New Testament books of the Bible.

God cannot be analysed, He is Spirit not matter, He has no physical weight, He cannot be felt, smelled, tasted, touched, or be seen by physical means or eyes. We are made in His Spirit image and likeness. This is why, I believe, many scientists reject God's existence. I believe there is no life greater than God's, who brought all other life into existence.

Are there any black people in heaven ?

I do not believe that there are, and for the following reasons. We are made in God's spirit image and likeness. Spirits do not have substance, no flesh. God knew us before we were born as spirit beings and knew us by our names before he put us together in our mother's tummy. His love is unconditional no matter what colour we are. The colour of the flesh dies with us.

I am a terrible worrier, what should I do ?

Your Adrenal gland says…without my 50,000 hormones, you would be dead in days - so help ensure my well being. My design allows that six times my weight of blood passes through me each minute. I am situated at the top of the kidney and without me you would be in a mess. You should not forget me. There is something you can or should do to ensure my well being. Avoid too much stress, worry, anger, hate as they are bad for me - so calm down a bit. Jesus says the same thing in (Matt 6/25-26-27-28 to 34) "Which of you by worrying can add one cubit to his life span ? ". The medulla was created in man by God to deal with stress. God made provision for these human conditions that man would experience and not be able to cope with, without the help of the Holy Spirit.

Was Darwin right about Evolution ?

I was told that Darwin had a conversion experience late in life and admitted his misgivings about evolution. Yet, to the present day, his writings, teachings and his beliefs are still taught in universities and schools all over the world. Some people I know, call it the Darwin guess. His theory may be right to some degree in the animal kingdom. I cannot accept that man is descended from the Apes. I believe man is the God of evolution. The missing link in Darwin's life before his conversion was God. (Ecclesiastes 7/29) says "That man was made upright" this could mean character or physical, Adam and Eve were honest upright people before the fall ? I believe it means both. (Geneses 1/27) says "So God created man in His own image; in the image of God He created him; male and female He created them". God the Father was never flesh. Jesus was God in the flesh, the second person of the Trinity and was born into time, because he lived outside of time. (Job 11/7-12) Gives me to understand that man can never find God searching in the sense realm. I believe when you have stretched yourself beyond the limits, the pride of the intellect will not let you go back and admit in public that you were wrong. (Psalm 9/17) "The wicket shall be turned into hell, all the nations that forgot God". (Isaiah 5/13-14) "Therefore my people will go into exile for lack of understanding; Their men of rank will die of hunger and their masses will be parched with thirst. Therefore the grave enlarges its appetite and opens its mouth without limit; into it will descend their nobles and masses with all their brawlers and revellers". (2 Cor. 4/3-4) "And even if our gospel is veiled, it is veiled to those who are perishing. The God of this age has blinded the minds of the unbelievers, so that they cannot see the light of the gospel of the glory of Christ, who is the image of God". The understanding of the Word is hidden to all who are not in Christ. (Jeremiah 29/13) "And you will seek Me and find Me, when you search for me with all your heart". I read in a book written by Dr. E. K. Victor Pearce, a Christian man, who is also an eminent scientist, archaeologist and theologian. whom I was honoured to meet. In volume I of his book, Evidence for Truth,. I read that Darwin had a conversion experience before he died. Dr Pearces' books are well worth reading and I believe should be in all schools, colleges and universities.

I read some where that I cannot recall that lies live on after the liar is dead, how true.

I have been in a relationship with a priest for five years; he keeps saying he will quit, hand in his notice and marry me; what do you think ?

I think you are mad. He like all men who cannot cope with chastity is going to use you and abuse you, if you allow him. I know from what other women in similar situations tell me, the minute you call home the promises of the love nest, he will start into a relationship with someone else, it happens all over the place. You become a sex object to fulfil his sexual needs. I have been told about midweek breaks and the foreign holidays. Rarely do they leave to get married, I doubt if your pal will marry you. Celibacy (not being married) he can live with, but cannot do without sex. The genuine priest or clergyman ordained by God, and there are thousands of them who need our support, will not get into such relationships. You are committing the sin of fornication, which is sex outside of marriage, he is a cheat who wants the best of two worlds. You need to repent, say the sinners prayer, get out, sue him for breach of promise, and report him to his Bishop! God loves both of you whether you love God or not. If either of you die without repenting you will end up in hell.

What does Gnosticism mean ?

Gnosticism, since its origins in or before the second century, has been rejected and condemned by the Christian churches. It refers to the secret doctrines and practices of mysticism where we could believe that we are of the same essence as God.

How do you pray against sickness ?

Do what Jesus did.

First of all, I believe before you pray with anyone, you must be empowered. You must be born again and be baptised in the Holy Spirit, you must have faith, Jesus says that we can do greater things than Him.

Simon's mother-in-law was suffering from a high fever, and they asked Jesus to help her. So he bent over and rebuked the fever, and it left her. She got up at once and began to wait on them. When I pray with someone, I ask God to bring the person closer to Jesus. By using the healing and conversion prayer on the last page of this book and asking God in Jesus name to rebuke the spirit of sickness or whatever, and fulfil the plan He has for the sick person by the power of the Holy Spirit, I believe this sickness will be healed.

What does the tribulation mean ?

This is spoken of in the book of Revelation. It means trouble or pressure of a general sort; in some passages, a particular time of suffering associated with events at the end of time. In this sense it is described as tribulation, surpassing any trouble YET experienced in human history, of misery, trouble, affliction and distress. We think we have experienced it all on earth prior to Christ's return but we do not know, we have to wait and see.

Is the devil real ?

He sure is, the Word mentions the devil in the New Testament approximately thirty six times.

I quote some:- Jesus was led by the Spirit into the desert to be tempted by the devil. The devil took him to the holy city. For forty days he was tempted by the devil. The devil said to him, "If you are the son of God, tell this stone to become bread".

He tells us that we belong to our Father the devil. We should not give the devil a foothold. Resist the devil, and he will flee. He is also called the ancient serpent. We should stand against the devil's schemes.

Just to mention a few quotes from Scripture about the devil, he tried to give Jesus a hard time, and did not succeed. Do not let him succeed with you. Tell him he has no future but you have, in Jesus' name. Adam and Eve failed the great test and plunged the whole human race into sin. Jesus was faithful. He became the Saviour of all who receive him. For confirmation read the following scriptures :- Matt 4/1 - 4/ 5 -Luke 4/2 - 4/3 Jn. 8/44 - James 4/7 - Rev.12/9.

Will I go to heaven when I die ?

I do not know, only God knows. Heaven is the fulfilment of the hopes of God's people those that are "born again" beyond this earthly life that is only temporary. To qualify, we must repent, feel regret for wrong deeds or omitting to do God's will. (Genesis 6/3-7) God said at one time "He was sorry he had created the human race, and that man would not live beyond 120 years". We must turn from sin to God and be born again, to receive the Spirit. It is a spiritual birth from above. (John 3/3) Jesus answered the man and said to him, "Most assuredly, I say to you, unless one is born again, he cannot see the kingdom of God". To be born again is an adult experience, I know, I am born again and have received the Spirit.

I have tried everything to give up smoking, can you help by praying with me ?

I usually go through the sinners prayer with people no matter what the problem and get them to ask for the gift of the Holy Spirit. Then ask the person to place their right hand under their chin, and ask God in Jesus' name, to remove from their taste buds the desire for nicotine. If there is a need or want in your emotions that you cannot identify, read the healing prayer on the last page of this book, as it covers most areas of the emotions. It is important to repent and seek the kingdom first, then healing can take place. I pray this way with people and it works.

Was Jesus baptized as a baby ?

No, he was registered, circumcised and presented as Joseph's and Mary's first born to God when they went to be registered for tax purposes in the Temple in Jerusalem.

Do I fulfil my duties as a Roman catholic by going to mass ?

No, and I quote from Vatican II Flannery edition on Priests page 545/ foot note 81 "A Christianity that is reduced to a mere fidelity to Mass - going is rejected ". I personally believe if you cannot love yourself and your neighbour, if you do not repent and be born again you will end up in hell. Fulfilling religious duties will not get you into heaven.

Who are the Mormons?

They are the church of Jesus Christ of Latter Day Saints. Founded by Joseph Smith (1805-1844). It is said he believed that neither Orthodox Christianity, Roman Catholicism, nor Protestantism were acceptable versions of Christianity, as they had all deviated to some degree from the purity of God's revelation in Jesus. The church is named after Mormon, an alleged prophet who lived in America in the fourth century of this era. The church split up when Smith died and the largest group went to Salt Lake City under the leadership of Brigham Young (1801-1877).

It is said that they practised polygamy until it was outlawed by the federal government in 1890. They believe that Adam and Eve are not responsible for our sin, that the book of Mormon has to be read along side the Bible, that family marriages and family last for eternity, that you must be self-reliant and that we can become God because they believe that God was once human.

A Mormon saying goes like this "What man is now, God was once; What God is now, man may become," Make up your own mind what you want to believe. Half of the 8-9 million Mormons in the world live in America. I stick with my Heavenly Father, who I can call Father, whose only Son Jesus, born of the Virgin Mary was crucified, died and was buried, and was raised on the third day by the power of God's Holy Spirit.

Do I have a list of saints, whom I could pray to for favours?

No, I do not. If you need a favour, as you put it, you first of all must learn how to pray so that God hears you. You must repent and be born again and ask God the Father in Jesus' name. We have this awful thing in Ireland, of praying to dead saints, dead people who may not be in heaven, only God knows who is. Jesus tells us how to pray and what to expect in the "Our Father". (In Romans 8/26 - 8/28) God tells us in His Word that it is the Spirit of Jesus within us that moans and groans for the things He knows we want before we ask. So you ask God the Father in Jesus' name to help you. Always remembering that repentance makes prayer worthy. When we pray to dead saints canonized by man we are calling on the dead to pray or help the living which is wrong. See page 354 in this book and read Iss. 8/19. It is the living saints, those that are empowered, born again and baptized in the Holy Spirit that pray for the living those in Christ who are in need.

What does the word Eucharist mean ?

It means thanksgiving, a word very much misunderstood I believe. I think we should call the mass a thanksgiving service. A joyous memorial proclamation of Jesus' finished work on Calvary.

What does the word mass mean?

The word mass means go forth with the good news you have just heard at mass. I could never have gone forth with the good news, I only knew it in Latin.

What do Muslims believe, my sister just recently married one ?

The Muslim religion is separated from the Christian religion by a huge void and is without doubt anti-Christian. The Islamic religion rejects the following from the Apostles' Creed. They reject God as Father. They reject His only Son, our Lord. They reject the fact that Jesus suffered under Pilate, was crucified died and was buried, and that he descended into hell and on the third day rose again from the dead and sits on the right hand of the Father, to judge the living and the dead.

* To sum it all up, they do not believe Christ died on the cross, and that Jesus was God's only Son. They believe that the Trinity is falsehood. However we must remember that God loves us all, Mormon, Muslim, Roman Catholic etc, no matter what doctrine you believe. The God I believe in, is God the Father of the Trinity, Jesus the Son and the Holy Spirit.

Why no women Priests or Evangelists?

(Page 186 /803)

The Catechism of the catholic church says "You are a chosen race, a royal priesthood, a holy nation, God's own people" this is confirmed in (1 Peter 2/9) and reads as follows "But you are a chosen generation, a royal priesthood, a holy nation. His own special people, that you may proclaim the praises of Him who called you out of darkness into His marvellous light". This message as far as I can understand has nothing to do with denominations, it has to do with being born again and being baptised in the Holy Spirit, and being empowered to do His work. There are priests and clergymen all over the world, ordained by man and not by God, who will end up in hell when they die, and so will a lot of the people they were to shepherd. Men of the corporate church will not encourage women priests. It is written in the Word that all who come to Jesus that are born of the Spirit from above (men or women no distinction) are a chosen people, a royal priesthood, a people belonging to God, as I have already quoted, that you may declare the praises of Him who called you out of darkness into to His wonderful light. You are now a people of God, once you had not received mercy, but now you have received mercy. All priesthood's die with us; Jesus was the only one that was ordained a priest forever.

The real church are the believers and they are scattered in all of the denominational churches and new churches. Death through Adam, Life through Christ. The Word says that God wants to pour out His Spirit on all men and women, like he did with the men and women at Pentecost. God did not say to my wife Dolores that she could not receive the Holy Spirit, when she called out His name and asked for the Holy Spirit, she received it. So can you like millions of other women in the world. If you invite Jesus into your life everything is possible. The gifts of the Spirit are available to all who ask, no exceptions. God does not need any of us but if we make ourselves available He will use us male or female, but you need to be empowered. The leaders of all the churches who restrict the use of the gifts, or encourage sectarianism will be called to account by God.

A friend of mine who was Roman Catholic said that we in the Roman Catholic Church, crucify Jesus again every time we attend mass, is this true ?

No, it is not true. Mass meaning go forth, is a sacrifice of praise and thanksgiving around the table of the Lord from the lips of those who know Jesus, it is not a "blood sacrifice". Jesus died once only, so that we might live forever in heaven.

I cannot forgive, I do good works etc. to make up for it in God's eyes, what do you think ?

It is not what I think, I can only tell you what it says in the prayer Jesus gave us, when He was asked we how should pray. The "Our Father" states that we must forgive those who trespass against us, just like God has forgiven us.

(John 20/23)

It is written in the Word and I quote "We are not to retain any sin of unforgiveness towards any person. Whose sins you shall forgive they are forgiven, whose sins you shall retain they are retained". You suffer if you cannot forgive.

I am separated for a few years now and in a sexually active relationship. Should I go to church and receive holy Communion, will I go to hell if I die ?

(1 Co. 11/27-28)

Yes, if you do not repent and be born again from above, just like anybody else. Jesus says "Therefore, whoever eats the bread or drinks the cup of the Lord in an unworthy manner will be sinning against the body and blood of the Lord . A man ought to examine himself before he eats of the bread and drinks of the cup". This is what you are doing, breaking a commandment and committing adultery. However, it does not stop God from loving you or your partner.

The God of my religion is not answering my prayers, despite my rosaries and all the candles lit, what should I do, any suggestions ?.

We are still at it in Ireland, when will we learn that God's love is a gift to be asked for and received, after repentance, you cannot receive it by doing holy things. All of these holy rituals are a complete waste of time. Read the prayer on pages 429-430 and invite Jesus into your life.

One of my children is in jail for robbing and

drug abuse, I cannot cope.

Mrs._____ said you would pray with me on the phone like you did with her, and she can cope ok now. *I asked the Mammy to follow me in the following prayer*

"Heavenly Father, I come to you in brokenness. You know my son is in jail, he has been a bad boy. However he is still my son and I love him. Help me believe as I say this prayer with John and open my eyes to understanding. I thank you for allowing these things happen to my son, (mammies sometimes make the following remark, "I never thought I would hear myself say that that"). Because I cannot cope I am calling out to you. John, who is praying with me said that when he called out, you answered, so please answer me in this my time of need. John and I seek your kingdom first. I repent for all my sins and ask you not to allow me retain any sin of unforgiveness towards any person, wash me heavenly Father with the precious blood of your

.

only son Jesus Christ, who I now accept as my Lord and Saviour. Having repented, I thank you for this trial I am going through, as it brings me closer to you my Heavenly Father, who brings me closer to Jesus. I ask now for the gift of the Holy Spirit, and I receive it. I ask you for an extra measure of faith to believe your Word and promises, that something good is going to come out of all this. I also ask for the gifts of wisdom and discernment to apply to my every day activities. Having repented I know you hear my prayer, as repentance makes prayer worthy.

"I ask you Heavenly Father in Jesus' name, to heal my son, remove from his mind all the hurts, anxieties and fears of the past that linger with him. I rebuke them all in Jesus' name. Lord, bring him closer to you. I leave him and myself under your protection from this moment on and know you will fulfill the plan you have for both of us. I thank and praise you in Jesus' name, Amen".

What is God like?

First of all, I believe that He is a person a spirit being, He is the substance of all human virtues, He is all - wise and all - knowing, He can do everything and anything we cannot do, He is everything good that we would like to be. He is all-powerful and infallible. God is good; He was and still is a place of safety for me when I turned to Him in my brokeness and trouble and can be for you also. He can be trusted to care for those who call on His name and will deliver them from bondage. We see His glory everywhere. He is not bound by human nature because He is God. He is the source of all life and everything in it; He is Lord of heaven and earth and does not dwell in temples made with hands and lives outside of time. His Word and promises are timeless, and are applicable in all situations of the (past) present and future. He is God the Father of the Trinity and my heavenly Father.

Explain Exorcism?

Acts 19/11-16-17-19 gave me an understanding of exorcism, where you seek to expel evil spirits from a person by religious means, and also helped me understand people with **multiple personalities.**

God did extraordinary miracles through my favourite apostle Paul, so that even handkerchiefs and aprons that had touched him were taken to the sick, and their illnesses were cured and the evil spirits left them. (I believe this can only happen, when Spirit filled living saints pray with people, dead saints canonized by man have no power, only God knows who is in heaven). Some Jews who went around driving out evil spirits tried to invoke the name of the Lord Jesus over those who were demon-possessed. They would say, "In the name of Jesus, whom Paul preaches, I demand you to come out." Seven sons of Sceva, a Jewish chief priest, were doing this. One day the evil Spirit answered them, "Jesus I know, and I know about Paul, but who are you?" Then the man who had the evil spirit jumped on them and overpowered them all. He gave them such a beating that they ran out of the house naked and bleeding. (also read page 265 in this book).

My son and daughter have joined the born again crowd, I am devastated.

Just say "Thank you Lord". However, the thing is that they do not have to leave the Roman catholic church when born again. We need people to be born again in the Roman Catholic Church and other churches, maybe then they might come alive if the Spirit moves. There are, as I have already said, no Protestants, Roman Catholics, Jews or Gentiles in heaven, only those that are born again. Let no one tell you, priest or pastor, that we are born again through infant baptism. You will not go to heaven when you die if you are not born again of the Spirit from above, so it is written. There are thousands and thousands of people in the Roman Catholic Church that are born again and can ignore the things that are not of the Spirit, don't let anyone tell you different. It has nothing to do with being a member of a church, it has to do with having a personal relationship with Jesus.

I am over weight and being bullied, what should I do ?

There are lots of people over weight all over the world. Are any members in your family over weight, do you eat too much of the wrong foods. What is the relationship with your mam and dad brothers and sisters like. Check all these out first. If it turns out that medically there is no reason for you to be overweight, then have a look at your self esteem. Learn to love yourself first and pray for the bullies by saying the following;- Heavenly Father, you put me together in my mother's womb. You knew me by my name before my mam and dad did and I thank you - (if you don't know your dad) - I never met my dad my earthly Father so I ask you my Heavenly Father, to be my Father. I ask you in Jesus name to fill the cavity of loneliness in me with your Holy Spirit as I repent for my sins and receive the Holy Spirit. I ask you my heavenly Father to bring me and the bullies closer to Jesus. (When this happens, you won't care what size you are or who sneers at you) They sneered at Jesus too. Ask God to bless all who jeer you, and rebuke any spirit of intimidation in Jesus' name as you ask him to fulfill the plan he has for you.

I am a twenty eight year old male and not sure which church is the right church ? Which God is the right one ? Did Jesus have brothers and sisters ?

I believe that there is one true church, it is not Protestant, Roman catholic, or any other denomination. It is the Church of the Creed, the one holy catholic apostolic church of which Jesus is rock and head, and made up of those "born again" of the Holy Spirit from above, followers of Christ. The denominations remind me of chandeliers, with some bulbs lighting and some not. Those lighting are "born again" believers. Those not lighting are dead to the Word of God like I was. The God I believe in, as a Christian, is God the Father of the Trinity who loves every human being unconditionally and wants to pour out His Spirit on all, no matter what God they believe in. The Catechism of the Catholic Church and Scripture also states in Luke 2/7 "Jesus was Mary's first born". Galations 1/19-Paul says "He did not see any other apostles, except James, the Lord's brother". No one really knows if Mary had other children after James. Invite Jesus into your life, say the healing and conversion prayer on page 429-430 now, and ask the Holy Spirit to direct you.

What is love?

I don't think that you can separate charity from love. 1 Corinthians 13/4-7 says the following. "Love is patient, love is kind. It does not boast, it is not proud. It is not rude, it is not self-seeking, it is not easily angered, it keeps no record of wrongs. Love does not delight in evil but rejoices with the truth. It always protects, always trusts, always hopes, always perseveres. Love never fails."

I have heard people say that God is love or that God is mercy, however I believe that God is God a Spirit being a person, and the things that I have just mentioned like Love and mercy are gifts from God, but are not God.

My son is gay, will he go to hell if he dies ?

We will all go to hell when we die if we are not born again of the Spirit from above. You must repent admit that you are sinner and invite Jesus to come live in you. It is an adult experience. I have said the same thing a few times in this book. It is no harm to have gay feelings or any kind of feelings. Lots of young people are confused and do have problems about their sexuality, by having good thoughts and bad. They can be led astray, by gay men, who are sexually active and who try to normalise their activities, by saying that lots of people are doing it and that it is normal.

Set out below is what God says, not what John Manning says in answer to the above question.

Sex between a man and a women outside of marriage is forbidden by God. You commit the sin of fornication. Sex between two men is also forbidden. The next paragraph tells us what Jesus says about sex between two men.

Leviticus Old Testament 18/22 "Do not lie with a man as one lies with a women; that is detestable". New Testament Romans 1/27 "In

414

the same way the men also abandoned natural relations with women and were inflamed with lust for one another. Men committed indecent acts with other men, and received in themselves the due penalty for their perversion.

(also read the following Scriptures in any Bible, Gen. 19/5 - 1Cor. 6/9 - 2 Peter 2/10 - Jude 8)

I believe you can pray yourself out of the darkness that this kind of activity draws you into.

***

In this book I am not telling people how they should live. God has given every human being the gift of free will to live their lives as he or she wishes. I have no right to say different. I answer questions that troubled people ask and use the Scripture to give the answers. God loves you actively gay or not. We are responsible to God for our actions and we will suffer the consequences of our actions no matter what sin we commit, if we do not repent and be born again before you die.

I have been married three times, which husband will I be with in heaven ?

John "I hope not the first one, he beat me up".

(Matt. 22/25-32 Romans 8/18-23)

Scripture says quite clearly that there are no husband and wife relationships in heaven and it is wrong to think that it is an extension of earth. I have often said to men and women that there will be no sexual activity in heaven. Some are delighted and some are disappointed and others do not care either way. No matter what your favourite activity was on earth, nothing can compare with what God has in store for us in heaven, where there will no longer be need for procreation and the necessity of mating and child nurture. We will all be brothers and sisters in Christ to live forever and ever, all one in Christ. Your closeness to Jesus will not save the members of your family, each person must have their own relationship with Jesus. The believers, those born again and in the Spirit can pray their friends and family into the kingdom of heaven.

Do you John Manning go to Mass anymore ?

I

LOVE GOING TO MASS NOW.

I AM NOT BORED LIKE I WAS

BEFORE MY CONVERSION.

I AM NOT SPIRITUALLY BLIND

OR DEAF ANYMORE.

I HAVE COME INTO THE KNOWLEDGE

OF THE WORD OF GOD. I UNDERSTAND

THE SCRIPTURES AND CAN SEPARATE

TRUTH FROM PIOUS OPINIONS.

* I always have a pencil with me at mass, and as the Scripture is read, I take notes as the Holy Spirit reveals understanding.

I am married and do not love my spouse. Life is a living hell. What can you suggest.

There are millions of married people who do not love their spouses who cope and get by every day. I believe that if you cannot love yourself you cannot love others. We can only love others by the grace of God and not in our own strength. It is written in the Word of God that hatred stirs up dissension. but love covers all wrongs.

We are made for eternity, the things of time cannot fully and permanently satisfy.

There is a time to love and a time to hate. The Word also says that the love of most will grow cold but he who stands firm to the end will be saved (go to heaven when you die). What you are going through is temporary, we are mortal after all. No man or woman can live beyond 120, so it is written. It is better to go through what you are going through, than lose your spirit body, that is a living soul to Satan and have to live with him and his gang forever and ever. You phoned because you are sad lonely and broken hearted and you needed a chat.

given on to you, focus on Jesus and follow me in the following prayer.

Father in heaven I have come to you in my brokenness. John and I come together on this modern telephone to share your Word, the living Word. Heavenly father I thank you for my children, and for my husband and the good years we have had together. I thank you for allowing us to have children that will populate heaven as spirit beings, in your time. I just seem not to love my husband anymore, and each day is a terrible struggle, but then so was your walk to the cross until you got some help. I need help now heavenly father and I ask you in Jesus' name as John and I pray together. I repent for all my sins from my head to my heart. Help me to forgive all who have hurt me and do not let me retain any sin of unforgiveness towards any person, particularly my husband the father of my children. You have known me, my husband and our children by our names while we were still in our mammy's tummy. As I repent for all my sins in Jesus' name, I now ask you for the gift of the Holy Spirit, the gift of faith, wisdom and discernment which I receive. The Spirit within me now is greater than the spirit of low self esteem and loneliness. I rebuke any spirit within me that is not of you in Jesus' name. Help me to love my husband unconditionally like you love me. Fulfill the plan you have for us as a family. I thank you for allowing this awful experience happen to me. When Jesus' comes live in you, you do not need anyone else. As I have already said in this book that Adam and Eve, Mary and Joseph, were able to love one another by the grace of God. Adam and Eve were never married publicly, but Mary and Joseph were. Lord what you have done for others you can do for me.

Why are there so many churches in the world?

I believe that for the Christian, there is only one true church. As I have already said in the text, it is not Protestant, Roman Catholic, Anglican, Methodist, Baptist, or any logo bearing group.

(Modern Catholic Encylopedia page 173 under the heading of Church the origin and history)

"The four Gospels frequently present Jesus surrounded by a group of disciples who have dedicated themselves to him and learn from him. There are also several indications that Jesus expected them to continue as a group after his death. Thus he gives them teachings, ministries, rituals, (I don't like the word ritual, rituals don't cause conversion) mission, and the promise of the future direction of the Holy Spirit. After Jesus' death, apostles and missionaries spread his message and established communities throughout the Mediterranean world and beyond". The Church then for me is where two or more are gathered in Jesus' name and as the circle gets bigger, it becomes the body of Christ. Each member should be guided by the Holy Spirit. I now live my life guided by the Holy Spirit and by the grace of God I can cope. If you are not guided by the Holy Spirit, I believe you are carnal.

Christians should share one life in Christ and be bonded together by the Holy Spirit. Sectarianism has caused the body to be broken in so many ways, which allowed the Word of God to be contaminated. The followers of Jesus should never have allowed Rome during the reign of Constantine to highjack and use the network they had set up. I believe that the reformation of the sixteenth century in its various aspects allowed splinter groups or churches to set up, with which came sectarianism and denominationalism.

John do you think that Roman Catholic priests should be married ?

I believe it should be his own choice. He should not be forced. I also believe that Paul was the only one of the Apostles that was not married, in fact it is thought that he was and that his wife died. One Corinthians 7/1 "Now for the matters you wrote about: It is good that you not marry. But since there is so much immorality, each man should have his own wife and each woman her own husband and each should fulfil his or hers marital duty to one another. All of chapter 7 to 40 should be read. Chapter 7/9 goes on to say that "If they cannot control themselves, they should, for it is better to marry than to burn with passion". I have already said else where in this book, that it is humanly impossible to cope with the sexual urges if you are not in the Holy Spirit.

Why do you do what you do?

I believe the following Old Testament story explains what I do as an evangelist by the grace of God. I bring empty broken vessels before Him and He fills them.

The story is in 2 Kings 1/7 and reads as follows.

The wife of a man from the company of the prophets cried out to Elisha, "Your servant, my husband, is dead and you know that he revered the Lord. But now his creditor is coming to take my two sons as slaves. Servitude as a means of debt payment by labour was permitted in Mosaic law and was greatly abused. The law limited the term of such bondage to six months but it could be twenty years. When the mammy was asked what she had in the house she said she had nothing except a little oil. Elisha said "Go around and ask all your neighbours for empty jars, don't just ask for a few. Then go inside and shut the door behind you and your sons. She left him and afterwards shut the door between her and her sons. They brought the jars to her and she kept pouring. When all the jars were full she said to her son. "Bring me another one". But he replied "There is not a jar left". Then the oil stopped flowing. She went and told the man of God, and he said, "Go, sell the oil and pay your debts. You and your sons can live on what is left".

When the Holy Spirit touches you, you want to tell others what Jesus has done and is doing in your life, without imposing yourself on others. Religion I believe can sometimes try to bring people to God before their time and fail miserably. In Acts 1/8 "Jesus says you will be my witnesses". I love being a witness and doing what I do, the Lord puts empty containers, broken people before each day were I either sow or water a seed that only God can make grow.

Why no rosary ?

Some people who have shared with me believe, that if you say the rosary you are pleasing God, and wonder why people in other churches do not say the rosary. I answered them by quoting from Page 570/ foot note 217 of the Flannery edition of Vatican II under the heading of priests, and a recommended form of prayer and priestly piety.

"Among the practices enumerated, one at first sight could be surprised by the omission of the rosary, but remember that Vatican II is a document intended for the priests of the whole church and in the Eastern Churches our Lady is honored by other prayer forms". I gather from what I have read that the rosary is not recommended as part of the prayer life for a Roman catholic priest. I personally believe that the rosary is a beautiful prayer except for the second part of the Hail Mary that was added to the Magnificat by a pious person and is not a truth. Why teach the rosary or recommend it as a prayer, if it is not acceptable to all believers. Saying the rosary will *NOT* cause or bring about conversion.

What is the millennium?

(Rev. 20/2-3)

I believe the present millennium, 1,000 years is self-explanatory. When Jesus comes back the biblical Millennium starts, it will be a period of peace, love, and brotherhood when all nature will live in harmony that was intended in the Garden of Eden. Only God knows when it will be. The book of Isaiah (11/6-9) speaks of a time when the wild animals will live at peace with domestic animals, when the serpents will no longer bite. A little child will be able to play in a Cobra's den or lead wild beasts around and not be harmed. Implements of war will not be used and all people will live in harmony. When this happens I believe it will be in the present earth's atmosphere, to let man see what it would be like had Adam and Eve not screwed up.

(Rev. 12/11)

*They overcame him (Satan) by the blood of the
Lamb and by the word of their testimony; they did
not love their lives so much as to shrink from death.*

******

The people of the abbreviated testimonies in this
book have come to Jesus as He says they should.

They have come out of darkness into the light.
They are happy and can cope. They know life will
not be easy, and if by chance they do things they
should not do and hit that pain barrier again in
that marathon of life, they know what name to
call on , do you ?

Luke 15/7

I believe the following Scripture applies to the stories of the people in this book

" In the same way, I tell you, there
will be more joy in heaven over one
sinner who repents than over
ninety nine - righteous persons who do
not need to repent".

The Healing and Conversion Prayer.

The Spirit of Christ living within you takes you from darkness into the light and is greater than the spirit of any of the conditions listed, that keeps you in bondage and darkness and prevents you from coping.

Emotions, Heart Disease, Cancer, Mental worries, Depression, Money worries, Broken relationships including marriage, Bereavement, Family suicide, Hate, Pride, Rejection, Loneliness, Diabetes, Gambling, Poor self image, Alcoholism, Arthritis, Migraine, Child abuse, Unforgiveness, Bad memory of parents or abusers, friends or family, Not letting go of children or others, Feeling unfulfilled, Guilt of any kind including abortion, Confusion about your sexuality. If your condition is not listed just add it on.

"Heavenly Father of the Trinity, you created my inmost being, you knit me together in my mother's womb. I praise you because I am fearfully and wonderfully made, your works are wonderful, I know that full well . I am not so well just now, as you know. I repent for all my sins, and ask your forgiveness through your only Son Jesus, whom I accept as my Lord and

Saviour. Help me to forgive all who have hurt me and send your Holy Spirit to those I have hurt. Comfort them so that they can forgive me. Jesus I know that repentance makes prayer worthy. I now claim the gift of your Holy Spirit and accept the first of the gifts. Give me an extra measure of faith, wisdom and discernment that I can apply to my every day life. Your Spirit within me is greater than the spirit of the world coming against me that keeps me in darkness*. I rebuke (this spirit, name condition) in Jesus' name. Jesus light up this darkness and set me free, so that you can fulfill the plan you have for me. Thank you heavenly Father in Jesus' name Amen. (composed by John Manning, while reading Psalm 139). Conversion is the greatest miracle of all. I believe if you can heal the emotions, you will heal and prevent a lot of sickness in the troubled world we live in.

* Read pages 183-187.

Could you answer any of the questions put to me in the question and answer section of this book ?

COULD YOU HELP ?

*

How would you pray with someone who might have one of the problems set out below ?

———————

With someone who has a drink problem and needs help ?

With a mammy who had an abortion, miss carriage or still birth ?

With someone who has a gambling problem ?

With someone depending on substances ?

With the families of suicide victims ?

With families who have had a loved one murdered ?

With parents of special needs children ?

With someone where love has grown cold ?

With someone whose prayers have never been answered ?

With a person who is afraid of dying and wants to know will they go to heaven when they die, or does it exist ?

With someone where mam, dad, child, brother or sister has died ?

With a person who has special needs child or adult ?

With a person, child, husband or wife that was subject to domestic violence ?

With a person who is ok on medication and not if they don't take it ?

Are we free ?

When women are raped.

When children and mam or dad are subject to domestic violence and are ignored.

When children are sexually abused by evil men and women lay and religious and ignored.

When old people cannot feel safe in their own homes.

When we cannot sleep at night and have to have massive security to protect our property.

When children cannot play any more without being supervised or have a personal minder.

When old and young are not safe walking the streets.

When young boys and girls become prostitutes.

When we need legislation to prevent divorce and abortion.

When the minders of special needs people are ignored.

When evil people of church and state try to normalise activities that breaks God's law and the law of the land.

When so many of our young people commit suicide.

When sexually transmitted diseases are rampant.

434

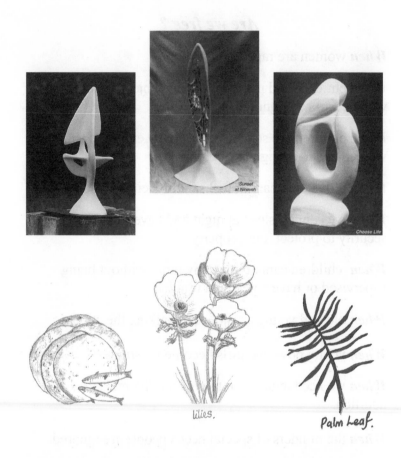

lilies.

Palm Leaf.

Paul and Catherine of the Testimonies in this book received Spiritual Gifts on top of the natural gifts displayed on this page.

THIS BOOK IS A GIFT

FROM

....

TO

....

DATE...............